TREES OF THE
PACIFIC NORTHWEST

Trees of the US

TREES OF THE
PACIFIC NORTHWEST

George A. Petrides

illustrations by Olivia Petrides

STACKPOLE
BOOKS

Published by
STACKPOLE BOOKS
5067 Ritter Road
Mechanicsburg, PA 17055
www.stackpolebooks.com

Printed in the United States of America

10 9 8 7 6 5 4 3 2 1

First edition

Originally published in 1998 by Explorer Press

Cover design by Wendy A. Reynolds
Illustrations on pages 6–9 reprinted from *A Field Guide to Western Trees*,
Houghton Mifflin Co., 1992
Map on page 103 based on Little (1971)

Library of Congress Cataloging-in-Publication Data

Petrides, George A.
    Trees of the Pacific Northwest / George A. Petrides ; illustrations by
Olivia Petrides.—1st ed.
        p. cm. – (Trees of the U.S.)
    "Originally published in 1998 by Explorer Press"—T.p. verso.
    Includes biographical references and index.
    ISBN 0-8117-3167-7 (pbk.)
    1.Trees—Northwest, Pacific—Identification. 2. Trees—Northwest,
Pacific—Pictorial works. I. Title. II. Series.

QK144.P48 2005
582.16'09795—dc22   2004058957

Here are the grandest forest-trees,

each a giant of its kind,

assembled together in one and the same forest,

surpassing all other coniferous forests in the world,

both in the number of its species

and in the size and beauty of its trees.

The winds flow in melody through their colossal spire

and they are vocal everywhere

with the songs of birds and running water.

—adapted from John Muir, *The Mountains of California,* 1913

Douglas-firs
Cathedral Grove, Vancouver Island,
Parksville, British Columbia

CONTENTS

FROM THE AUTHOR

The world's finest stands of redwoods, spruces, firs, hemlocks, and other coniferous trees blanket the coastal slopes and islands of the Pacific Northwest from Oregon to central Alaska. Whether cruising the Inside Passage or traveling overland, one cannot fail to be thrilled by the magnificent timberlands, enchanting streams, waterfalls, lakes, and mountain peaks that extend inland to the Rocky Mountains. Due in large part to the tree species that clothe these incomparable landscapes, the Pacific Northwest comprises a wonderland that attracts visitors from around the world.

I first became interested in the identification of trees and shrubs while studying the food preferences of deer during their critical winter season. It was important to identify not only the twigs browsed by deer but also those that the animals neglected or avoided as food. Even though leaves were absent, I had to identify these plants quickly while snowshoeing along cruise lines through the forest. Ever since then, I have tried to detect or confirm field marks that would easily identify a woody plant at any season, not just when flowers, fruits, or even leaves were present.

Acknowledgments

Judge James B. Strong, a keen naturalist of Olympia, Washington, has been most helpful in advising on the status of tree species in the Pacific Northwest, in providing several botanical specimens, and in reviewing the manuscript of this work. His friends, retired U.S. Forest Service forester Jim Riley of Randle, Washington, and Dr. Lou Messmer, Professor Emeritus at Grays Harbor College, Aberdeen, Washington, also kindly reviewed the manuscript and offered helpful suggestions. These several experts serve as inspired members of the Washington Plant Society.

Dr. Gustaaf A. de Zoeten, Professor and Chairman of the Department of Botany, and Dr. Alan Prather, Curator, graciously made available the fine collection of Pacific Northwest plants that forms a part of the Michigan State University herbarium. I am grateful, too, to Dr. Stephen N. Stevenson, Associate Professor of Botany at Michigan State University, and Kathleen Ahlenslager of the U.S. Forest Service, who suggested improvements in the text.

My daughter, Olivia, Adjunct Professor at the School of the Art Institute of Chicago, provided the clear artwork for this book and others in this series. She also painted the color illustrations for our more comprehensive *Field Guide to Western Trees*. I wish to express my sincere appreciation to her for her fine work.

An Important Note

There are indications in this book that fruits and other parts of certain plants reportedly have been used for food or medicinal purposes. Although this information has been gleaned from reputable sources, it is included here for general interest and has *not* been verified as being absolutely true. Do not eat or take internally any part of a plant for any purpose unless it has been confirmed by an expert that it is safe to do so.

As well, this book notes that some plants were once used to disable and catch fish—a practice that today is illegal and certainly unsportsmanlike.

The forests of the Pacific Northwest are national treasures. It is illegal to collect plants for any purpose in national and state parks of the region and on many other lands without a permit. Please help to preserve our beautiful forests!

HOW TO USE THIS BOOK

This book is designed for in-the-field use. It provides guidelines that will help the observer identify any tree that grows wild in the Pacific Northwest in any season, not just when the tree is in leaf or in flower. All 134 native or naturalized trees in the region are covered. These trees are divided into 40 small groups comprised of species that look alike whether or not they are actually related. Within each group, similarities and differences are pointed out.

The following chart (also shown on the book's back cover) will help you locate illustrations and information about the tree you are trying to identify. To use the chart, decide which statement 1 is true, then which statement 2 is true, and so on, until the appropriate section is reached.

1. Leaves needlelike or scalelike
   (conifers)   **Section I, Plates 1–14**
1. Leaves broad
   2. Leaves opposite or whorled
      3. Leaves compound   **Section II, Plates 15–16**
      3. Leaves simple   **Section III, Plates 17–20**
   2. Leaves alternate
      4. Leaves compound   **Section IV, Plates 21–22**
      4. Leaves simple   **Section V, Plates 23– 40**

To use this chart, you must first be familiar with the meaning of some common descriptive terms, beginning with the difference between opposite, whorled, and alternate leaves. Opposite leaves occur in pairs, and the leaves are positioned directly across from each other on a twig. Whorled leaves are the same as opposite leaves, except there are three or more leaves ringing the twig. Alternate leaves are staggered along opposite sides of a twig; they are not directly across from each other. Remember that when leaves are absent, a specimen can still be categorized as alternate, whorled, or opposite by the positions of the leaf scars and buds.

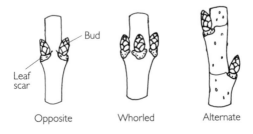

Opposite   Whorled   Alternate

The chart also differentiates between simple and compound leaves. A simple leaf has a single broad blade with a central midrib. The basal, or lowermost, portion of the midrib forms the leafstalk, which is attached to the twig. (The leafstalk is for the most part not woody and can be easily detached from the woody twig.) A compound leaf also has a midrib, but a number of separate leaflets are attached to it.

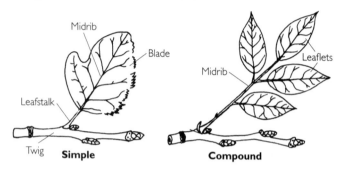

Simple · Compound

Compound leaves can be further identified as feather-compound, fan-compound, or twice-compound, according to the arrangement of the leaflets.

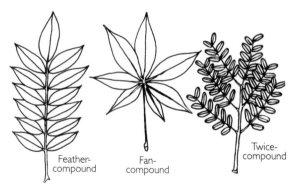

Feather-compound · Fan-compound · Twice-compound

When a leafstalk separates from the twig, it leaves a leaf scar that contains tiny dots, known as bundle scars, that can be seen easily with a hand lens; a bud also normally remains nearby. But when a leaflet becomes detached from a midrib only an indefinite mark of attachment is evident and no bud is present.

Bud · Bundle scar · Leaf scar

In this book, "twig" refers only to the end portion of a small branch, the part that constitutes the newest growth. A branchlet is the previous year's growth, separated from the twig by a series of encircling end-bud scars. "Branchlet" is also used here to mean any small branch that is not a twig. Short branchlets with closely positioned leaves and leaf scars are known as spur branches.

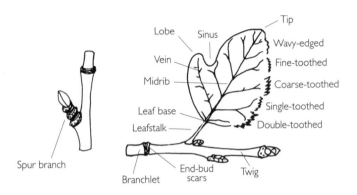

Other useful identifying features are the shape of the leaf edge; the number of bud scales and bundle scars; and the characteristics of the buds, pith, and leaf and stipule scars. The drawings on the next page illustrate these features.

This book follows the U.S. Forest Service definition of a tree: a woody plant at least 13 feet tall with a single trunk at least 3 inches in diameter at breast height. Trees not described as evergreen can be assumed to be deciduous. Within the text botanical terms are avoided; simple language is used throughout. Nevertheless, scientific as well as common names are given so that descriptions in other books can be compared.

Identifying Unknown Trees
Collecting plants for identification and study is a practice that has long been sanctioned by science. Collections should be made, however, only in moderation and under suitable conditions. Wild plant collection must be balanced against the need to preserve natural values. Also, remember that in some areas, including national and state parks and monuments, it is illegal to collect plants without a permit.

Remember, too, that it is often easier to make an accurate identification in the field than it is to make one from a collected specimen. A number of important characteristics—milky

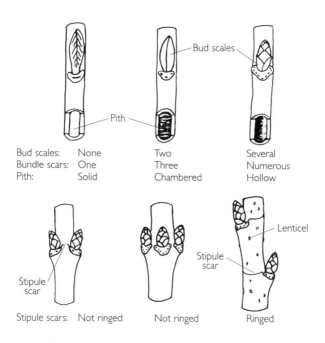

Bud scales:	None	Two	Several
Bundle scars:	One	Three	Numerous
Pith:	Solid	Chambered	Hollow

Stipule scars:	Not ringed	Not ringed	Ringed

sap, spicy odors, bark pattern, growth habits, and fallen leaves and fruits—are more obvious when you examine a whole living tree than they are when you look at a collected specimen.

If you do want to collect a specimen for later study and it is appropriate to do so, keep in mind that a good specimen is essential for correct identification. Avoid twisted, dwarfed, and gnarled branches. From a vigorous branch, clip from six inches to a foot of the branch tip so that both leaf and twig characteristics are present.

With the unknown tree or specimen at hand, use the chart to lead you to the proper section of this book, then scan the plates in that section to find the species that most resembles your tree. When leaves are absent, use the leafless key on pages 96–97 as well as the plate illustrations and text descriptions.

Fortunately, the field identification of trees requires a minimum of equipment: only a field guide and a hand lens are needed. A good hand lens is as essential to the botanical naturalist as binoculars are to the birder. Suitable hand lenses can be found at nature centers or any other place that sells optical equipment. A lens that magnifies 6x to 10x will not only disclose the beauty hidden in small blossoms but will be of great help in checking on the hairiness of leaves and twigs, the presence or absence of leafstalk glands, and other tiny details. Holding the lens close to your eye makes it almost part of you and usually enhances your field of vision.

Plant Names

In this book, common names that include the name of another unrelated group—Douglas-fir or Redcedar, for example—are either hyphenated or joined together to indicate that they are not true members of the group.

Although common names are well established for some species, such names often vary from one part of the country to another—and from one book to another. Because of this, scientific names are used to provide a standardized designation for a given species.

Scientific names have three essential parts: the name of the genus (plural *genera*), the name of the species (plural *species*), and the name, often abbreviated, of the botanist or botanists who assigned the name and stand as the authority behind it. Of the two Latinized terms, only the first name (the generic) is capitalized. An example is the scientific name for Pacific Dogwood: *Cornus nuttallii* Audubon.

Unfortunately, scientific names also may change as continued study indicates that a species is more closely related to members of a different group, that plants once thought to be two separate species should be combined as varieties of one species, or that a species originally thought to be new has already been named, and so forth.

Explaining the complicated rules of scientific nomenclature is beyond the scope of this book. To the amateur naturalist the principal value of scientific names is to ensure accuracy when seeking additional information about a species in other books. If both the Latin name and its authority agree, then the two books are presumably discussing the same species.

Scientific names tend to be anglicized when spoken. Don't hesitate to use them. In fact, if you call a certain plant an arbutus, a rhododendron, or a yucca you are already using scientific names. (In speech, the authority's names are usually omitted.)

The Flora of North America, now in development, is becoming the basic reference for plant names and classification. The scientific names accepted by the specialists who compiled the first volumes of this continuing series are used in this book. For species not yet covered by that guide, two sources are utilized. For Pacific Northwest trees that also occur in California, the names of Hickman (1993) and his collaborators are adopted. For other PNW species, the names listed are mostly those of Little (1979). Full citations are given in the References section.

Unless markedly distinctive in the field (Shore Pine or Lombardy Poplar, for example) or with names useful in cross-referencing, varieties or subspecies are not emphasized here. For full citations of references, see page 98.

Measurements
Where appropriate in the text, measurements are given for tree height, leaf and bud size, and other characteristics. Trunk widths are for the diameter at breast height, commonly $4^1/2$ feet above the ground, which foresters note as "d.b.h." Measurements are given in English units. For metric conversions, see page 103.

Environmental Factors
The aggregation of trees that occurs in any locality is determined first by the parent species present and then largely by the interacting factors of climate, soil, and other living things. Temperature and precipitation affect the survival of each tree species (especially that of seedlings) and also determine the characteristics of the soil upon which trees depend for much of their nutrient intake. Other plant and animal species may cause competition, disease, parasitism, browsing, and so on.

Differences in altitude cause climates, soils, and vegetation to vary greatly between locations. Tree floras in the mountains only a fraction of a mile apart may be quite different from each other and, in consequence, support different animal populations.

Plants that grow at low elevations in northern regions of North America are often found at high altitudes further south. A person ascending a high mountain may pass through several vegetative zones, each with its own characteristic tree species, before finally reaching timberline and alpine tundra near the top.

When you find and identify a tree that is new to you it is interesting to think about the environmental factors that enable its survival, and those that are likely limiting its distribution and abundance. Shallow soil, snow depth in winter, competition from other plants, excess soil moisture, drought, lack of soil fertility, fire, insect damage—all can keep a species from becoming more plentiful. Erosion, overuse, and pollution are human factors that can have powerful effects on a species' survival. As well, glacial or other geographic events might have brought the plant to its present distribution, or prevented its spread.

Exactly which environmental factors are affecting a specific tree cannot always be identified. Insight may come, however, as you examine other specimens at different locations. It is certain that some combination of climatic, soil, biotic, and historic factors has determined the current status of the species and will continue to influence its welfare.

Subalpine Firs
Olympic National Park, Washington

I. Trees w/ Evergreen Needle- or Scale-like Leaves

The forests of the Pacific Northwest display what may be the world's finest collection of coniferous trees. As shown on Plates 1-14, foliage, cones, and seeds can assist in the identification of conifers. If seeds are not visible between cone scales, cones can be placed in a paper bag and allowed to dry. The seeds then usually shake loose. Cone-bearing trees are often referred to as *softwoods*, in contrast to broadleaf or *hardwood* trees (Plates 15-40). While all conifers in the PNW are evergreen (except larches, Plate 5), some broadleaf trees (Section V) also retain their foliage throughout the year.

1. 5-NEEDLE PINES: Needles 2 1/2"- 4"Long

The pines of Plates 1 and 2 have *five* slender needles tied in bundles at the base by *short* (under 1/16") sheaths. The cones are *not* prickly. Five-needle pines are called *white* or soft pines because of the color of the wood and the ease with which it is worked.

The pines of this plate occur mainly on western slopes. Both have blue-green needles 2 1/2"- 4" long and otherwise much alike. Trunk bark and cones offer the best field marks. Cones are *long-stalked*. Look for them at the tips of high branches and on the ground nearby.

WESTERN WHITE PINE *Pinus monticola* Dougl. ex D. Don
The *dark* trunk bark of mature trees is broken into a shallow *checkered* pattern of small squarish pieces (photo p. 54). Younger trees have a smoother dark bark with a suggestion of being checkered. Cones slender, *4"- 10"* long, and with scales *1/2"- 3/4"* wide. The seed wing is *slightly* wider than the seed and has an angled or *pointed* tip. To 100'- 165' (235') tall and 3'- 5' (7') in diameter. A handsome tree rather thinly scattered in forests of the Sierra Nevada, Cascade, and coastal ranges and also in the Rocky Mountains of ne. Oregon /ne. Washington /nw. Montana to cen. British Columbia. Some trees live for 200-500 years. The clear wood has many commercial uses. It is the main source of materials for wooden matches.

SUGAR PINE *Pinus lambertiana* Dougl.
This elegant pine is the world's largest and with the longest cones. The trunk bark is *brown or gray* with deep *vertical ridges.* Cones are *10"- 18" (24")* long with scales *1"- 1 1/2"* wide. The seed wing is *considerably* wider than the seed and *rounded* at the tip. Height to 220'; diameter to 6' (8'). Found in the Pacific Northwest only west of the Cascades in w. Oregon. Also in the Sierra Nevada. Deep soils, 2500'- 9000' elevations. Some trees live for 600 years. Sugary nodules form at trunk wounds.

PLATE 1

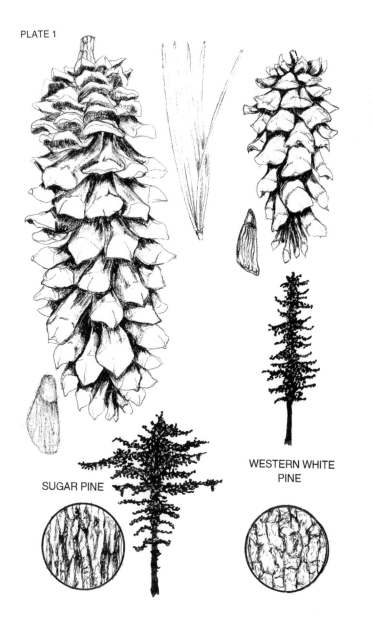

SUGAR PINE

WESTERN WHITE
PINE

2. 5-NEEDLE PINES: Needles 1"- 2 1/2" Long

In contrast to the species of Plate 1, these white pines have *shorter* needles and *smaller* cones, with stalks short or *absent* . Like the first group, however, the needles have *short* sheaths and the cones are *without* prickles. They are found often at high elevations north to cen. British Columbia. Lumber values are low.

LIMBER PINE *Pinus flexilis* E. James
  A high-altitude pine with needles 1 1/2"- 2 1/2" (3") long and twigs very flexible. Cones are *elongate, 3"- 6"* in length, *light brown*, the scales slightly thickened and *round-tipped*. Cones *open readily* when ripe. Seeds red-brown, *dark-mottled*, about 1/2" long, with narrow papery wings or none. Trunk bark brownish to black, furrowed. Height 35'- 50' (80'); diameter 1'- 2' (3'). Though presumably named for its flexible twigs, those of Whitebark Pine also can be twisted into knots. Mainly a species of the central and southern Rocky Mountains; in the PNW found from ne. Oregon, se. Idaho, and w. Montana to se. British Columbia and sw. Alberta. Mostly at 5000'- 12000' elevations on eastern slopes. It is a common tree and the only pine in Craters of the Moon National Monument, Idaho.

WHITEBARK PINE *Pinus albicaulis* Engelm.
  A timberline tree or shrub with needles and twigs much like those of Limber Pine. Cones, however, are *1"- 3"* in length, *dark purple, ± spherical*, with *thick, pointed* scales. Cones *remain closed even at maturity*, whether or not they fall. These cones, however, are mostly destroyed by birds, chipmunks, or squirrels. Clark Nutcracker, a large black and gray bird of the high country, is especially active in seeking the *wingless* nutlike seeds. Even if only fragments of purple cone scales are nearby, they may help to identify the plant. Trunk bark shows gray to whitish plates but, despite the name, is not distinctive. Height 15'- 30' (60'); diameter 1'- 2' (3'). Occurs at 7000' -12000' elevations from cen. California, ne. Nevada, and nw. Wyoming north to cen. British Columbia and w. cen. Alberta. Maximum length of life is believed to be 250-350 years.

PLATE 2

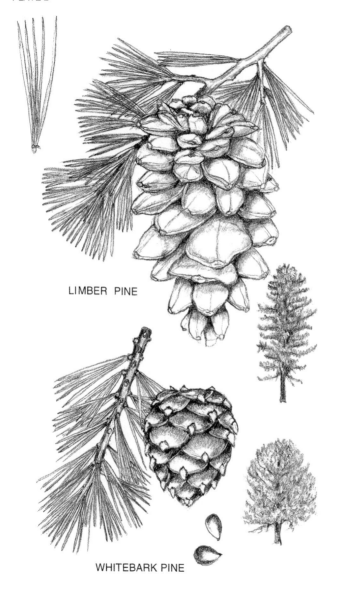

LIMBER PINE

WHITEBARK PINE

3. PINES with THREE NEEDLES per BUNDLE

Three pine species in the Pacific Northwest have *three* needles per bundle, each bundle bound by a sheath *1/4"- 1"* long. Cones are egg-shaped, *prickly* or thorny, and mostly short-stalked. Pines with two or three needles per bundle (Plates 3-4) are termed *yellow* or hard pines. Most are important for lumber, but the wood is pitch-filled and not as suitable for fine work as that of white pines.

PONDEROSA PINE *Pinus ponderosa* Dougl. ex Lawson
  The most widespread western conifer, one whose distribution is sometimes said to outline the American West. A large pine with 5"- 10" needles, usually *three* per bundle but sometimes, especially in the Rockies, only two; bundle sheaths 1/2"- 1" long. Cones egg-shaped, *3"- 6"* long, *dull* brown, the scales *dark* brown beneath and tipped with a slender, 1/8"- 3/16" long prickle often *curved out.* Seed 3/8"; wing 1" long. Mature bark in *yellow* plates faced with *flaky* jigsawlike pieces. Young trunks dark, rough. Height 60'- 130' (230'); diameter 2'- 4' (6'). Sunny sites to 5000'- 6000' elevations, north to cen. British Columbia. Various grouse and quail eat the seeds, mule deer browse the twigs, and porcupines gnaw the inner bark. Native Americans used the seeds for food and the pitch to waterproof woven containers. A very important lumber species.

JEFFREY PINE *Pinus jeffreyi* Grev. & Balf.
  Much like Ponderosa Pine and at one time combined with it. Needles 5"- 10" long with 1/4"- 1/2" sheaths. Cones *6"- 8" (10")* long, *shiny,* with scales *light* brown beneath, and at least the lower prickles mostly *turned in.* Seed 1/2"; wing 1 1/2" long. Mature trunks *not* flaky but *tightly furrowed,* rosy or *purplish-colored*, and with a pleasant *vanilla odor* (sniff in a furrow). Height 100'- 130' (180'); 2'- 4' (6'). Mostly at 6000' -9000' elevations, range extending from Baja California to sw. Oregon. John Jeffrey was an early Scottish botanical explorer.

KNOBCONE PINE *Pinus attenuata* Lemm.
  A small, often straggling, tree with *tightly closed* cones often clustered around a branch and *embedded* in the outer bark. Needles 3"- 6" long; sheaths 1/8"- 1/2" (7/8") in length. Cones *one-sided,* yellow-green, *curved,* 3"- 7" long. Some scales swollen, with prickly *knobs.* Seeds seldom released until cones are opened by fire. Trunk sometimes forked. Height 20'- 30' (80'); diameter 6"- 12" (24"). Low elevations, from n. Baja California to sw. Oregon. Lumber of little value.

PLATE 3

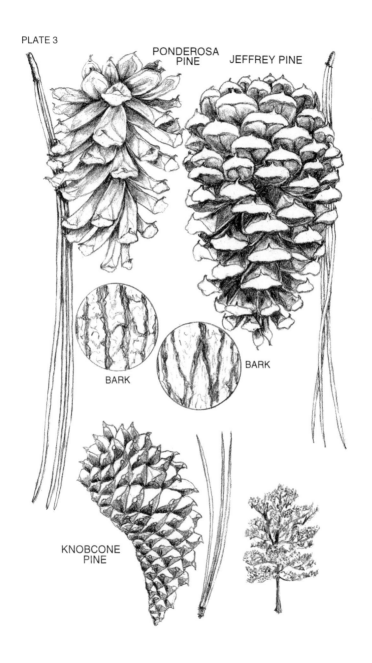

PONDEROSA
PINE

JEFFREY PINE

BARK

BARK

KNOBCONE
PINE

4. PINES with ONE / TWO NEEDLES per BUNDLE

In the Pacific Northwest, the first three pines of this plate regularly have needles in pairs. Ponderosa Pine (Plate 3) sometimes also may be two-needled. Singleleaf Pinyon has one needle "per bundle".

LODGEPOLE /SHORE PINE *Pinus contorta* Dougl. ex Loud.

Inland, Lodgepole Pine (vars. *latifolia* and *murrayana*) is a *tall, narrow-crowned* tree with short needles and small cones, reproducing in dense stands especially after a forest fire. Needles *yellow-green,* only *1"- 2" (3")* long, with sheaths just 1/16"- 1/8" (3/16") in length. Cones 1"- 2" in length, often *persisting* on the tree, scales thin and *prickly.* Mature trunk mostly with *thin, scaly, cornflakelike,* yellowish bark. Height 60'-100' (115'); diameter 1'- 2' (3'). Occurs at 3000'- 11,000' elevations from s. California and n. New Mexico to se. Alaska and cen. Yukon. Seeds eaten by squirrels and grouse, twigs browsed by deer, the inner bark gnawed by porcupines. Logs and lumber used in home construction. Native Americans once used sapling trunks for their teepee lodges.

In coastal areas, Shore Pine (var. *contorta)* has quite a different appearance. It is a *short, round-topped* tree with dense, *dark* needles. While its upland relative mostly has foliage only on branchlets that grew during the previous 1- 2 (4) years, Shore Pine branches offer a *foxtail* appearance with needles covering the preceding 3-7 (or more) years' growth. The trunk bark, too, is tightly *furrowed* and *blackish.* Height 15'- 30'; diameter 1'- 2'.

JACK PINE *Pinus banksiana* Lamb.

An often-straggly tree with needles yellow-green, only *1"- 1 1/2"* long, and sheaths as in Lodgepole Pine. Cones 1 1/2"- 2 1/2" long, strongly curved or *bulged* on one side. Cones open and release seeds mostly as a result of fires. Height ± 15'- 40'. Distributed widely across Canada and the n. United States, reaching the PNW only in extreme ne. British Columbia.

AUSTRIAN PINE *Pinus nigra* Arnott

A European tree widely planted and spreading in the Pacific Northwest. Needles *dark* green, rather stiff, *3"- 6"* long, with 1/4"- 1/2" (3/4") basal sheaths. Winter end buds *whitish.* Cones 2"- 3" long and *not* persistent; scale prickles ± 1/16" long. Seed 1/4"- 3/8"; wing 1/2"- 3/4". Mature trunk with *grayish-yellow* vertical bark plates. Resistant to pollution and sea air.

SINGLELEAF PINYON *Pinus monophylla* Torr. & Frem.

A nut pine with only *one* needle, 1"- 2 1/4" long, stout, *spine-tipped,* with a short, deciduous, papery sheath. Cone 2"- 3" long, ± globular, thick-scaled, and *thornless.* Height to 40'. Arid soils. Ranging north through the Great Basin to se. Idaho. Nuts were an important food for early native peoples and are still in demand.

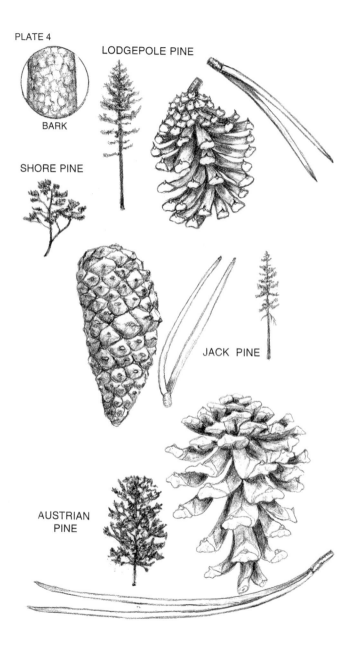

PLATE 4

BARK

LODGEPOLE PINE

SHORE PINE

JACK PINE

AUSTRIAN PINE

5. NEEDLES PINELIKE: Larches / True Cedars

The larches and true cedars of this plate resemble pines in having slender, needlelike foliage and woody cones. Unlike pines, however, they have many needles *clustered* on short spur branches and *single* needles on longer shoots. The cones have thin scales and are not prickly. Both groups are members of the pine family.

LARCHES are trees of cold climates that, unlike most conifers, are *deciduous,* the needles turning bright yellow in autumn before dropping. Knobby spurs remain on the branchlets. Larch cones are small and fall from the tree *as a unit.* Lumbermen are said often to have misnamed Silver Fir (Plate 9) as "larch".

WESTERN LARCH (TAMARACK) *Larix occidentalis* Nutt.
A tall narrow-crowned tree with short branches and sparse foliage. Needles 1"- 1 3/4" long and twigs *smooth, shiny.* Cones *1"- 1 1/2"* long with *pointed* bracts protruding from between the ± papery scales. Trunk often free of branches for half its height, the bark red-brown, *thick,* ridged, and fire-resistant. Height 100'- 180' (240'); diameter 3'- 4' (8'). The largest of all larches and a valuable timber species. 2000'-8000' elevations in the Cascades of Oregon /Washington and from ne. Oregon /cen. Idaho /nw. Montana to se. British Columbia.

SUBALPINE LARCH *Larix lyalli* Parl.
An often gnarled and twisted tree of the Pacific Northwest on slopes from 5000' to timberline. Needles 1"- 1 1/2" long; twigs *white-hairy.* Cones *1 1/2"- 2"* long, with *ragged* protruding bract tips. Bark *thin.* Height 30'- 50' (90'); diameter 1'- 3' (6'). Ranges across the international border in the Cascades and again in the Rockies of cen. Idaho /w.Montana /sw. Alberta.

TAMARACK (AMERICAN LARCH) *Larix laricina* (DuRoi) K. Koch
With needles *3/4"- 1"* in length and twigs *hairless,* this larch ranges from cen. Alaska, e. Yukon, ne. British Columbia, and w. cen. Alberta east to the Atlantic Ocean. Cones *1/2'- 3/4"* long with *no* visible bracts. To 80' tall on moist sites; often stunted.

TRUE CEDARS (*Cedrus* spp.) are imported species planted in landscaped areas mainly near the coast. Needles slender and clustered on spur branches like larches, but *evergreen* with cones *upright.* Cone scales are wide and *fall apart.* **Deodar Cedar** (*C. deodara* Loud.) of the Himalayas has *twigs and topmost leader shoot drooping.* It has leaves *1"- 2"* long, twigs hairy, and cones 3"- 5" long. Twigs do *not* droop in **Atlas Cedar** (*C. atlantica* Man.) of North Africa with needles *1/2"- 1"* long, twigs hairy, and cones *2"- 3"* long, or in **Cedar of Lebanon** (*C. libani* Loud.) with foliage 1"- 1 1/4" long, twigs *hairless,* cones 3"-4" in length.

PLATE 5

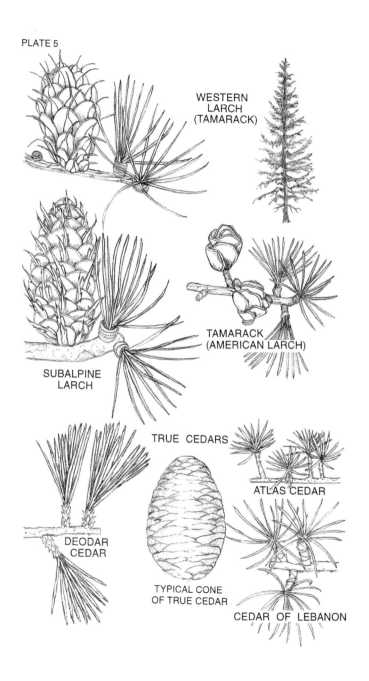

WESTERN
LARCH
(TAMARACK)

SUBALPINE
LARCH

TAMARACK
(AMERICAN LARCH)

TRUE CEDARS

ATLAS CEDAR

DEODAR
CEDAR

TYPICAL CONE
OF TRUE CEDAR

CEDAR OF LEBANON

6. NEEDLES on WOODY PEGS: Spruces I

Spruces have *single* needles on *small, stout, woody pegs* (seen best on dead twigs). Hemlocks (Plate 12), our only other trees to possess them, have only weak pegs. Spruces typically have *4-sided* needles that can easily be twirled between the fingers. Nevertheless, the first two species (on this plate) have *flattened* (and white-striped) needles that cannot be twirled.

Spruce needles are mostly *stiff,* pointed, and sometimes prickly. They grow all around the twig, and drop quickly upon drying. Spruce twigs are mostly hairless (remove needles and use lens). Cones are brown and woody, with papery scales and *no* prickles. Trunk bark is brown and *scaly.*

Spruce wood is soft, light, straight-grained, and useful for many purposes. It is a principal source of pulp for making paper. The inner bark has been ground and added to flour in bad times. Spruce beer reportedly can be made from fermented needles and twigs boiled with honey. Several species are used in landscaping.

SITKA SPRUCE *Picea sitchensis* (Bong.) Carr.
A coastal tree with *drooping,* hairless twigs and flat needles that are *prickly-sharp,* dark green, *white-striped,* and 3/4"- 1" long. Cones 2"- 4" long, with scale tips somewhat narrowed and ± *ragged.* Trunk bases of large trees are often swollen and *buttressed.* Height 100'- 160' (215'); diameter 3'- 4' (17'). Truly a tree of the Pacific Northwest, a resident of the fog belt from n. Calif. to s. Alaska. Our largest spruce. Some logs have resonant qualities valued for musical instruments. May live for 700-800 years.

WEEPING SPRUCE *Picea breweriana* Watson
An uncommon tree of the Siskiyou and nearby mountains of the Oregon /California border. Much like Sitka Spruce but with thin branches that hang *weeping* up to 8' long and with cone scales *broadly rounded* and *not* ragged. Twigs are *hairy.* William Brewer of Yale University discovered the species in the 1800s.

ENGELMANN SPRUCE *Picea engelmannii* Parry ex Engelm.
The principal spruce of inland mountains (except the Sierra Nevada) north to cen. British Columbia. Needles dark- to blue-green, *4-sided,* ± flexible, only moderately sharp. Twigs ± fine-hairy. Cones 1/2"- 2" (3") long, with scale tips *ragged* and extending *1/4"- 3/8"* beyond the seed wing impression. Height 80'- 100' (180'); diameter 1'- 3' (8'). A major lumber tree, sometimes with resonant logs. George Engelmann was a 19th century physician and botanist. See Blue/White spruces, Plate 7.

PLATE 6

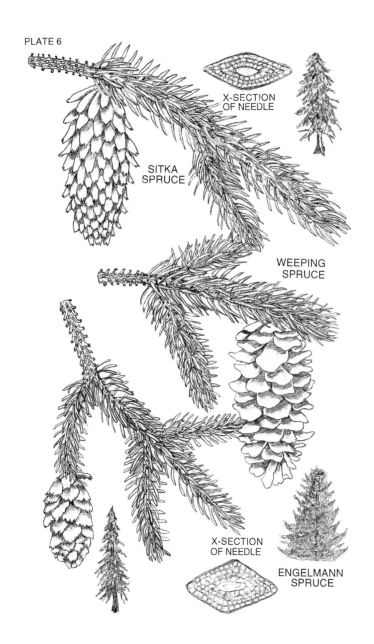

X-SECTION
OF NEEDLE

SITKA
SPRUCE

WEEPING
SPRUCE

X-SECTION
OF NEEDLE

ENGELMANN
SPRUCE

7. NEEDLES on WOODY PEGS: Spruces II

None of these spruces is native in either Washington or Oregon and Blue Spruce extends its range northward only into se. Idaho. White and Black spruces are distributed across most of Alaska / Canada as well as over parts of the northeastern and north-central lower 48 states. They are cold-hardy species that grow north to the limit of trees. These species all have *4-sided* needles. For the general characteristics of spruces, see Plate 6.

BLUE SPRUCE *Picea pungens* Engelm.
A species much like Engelmann Spruce (Plate 6) and often difficult to distinguish from it. The needles are *sharp;* twigs are *hairless;* cones are *2"- 4"* long with scale tips *ragged* and extending *1/8"- 1/4"* beyond the seed wing impression. The trunk bark tends to be *darker* and thicker than that of Engelmann Spruce. Foliage is green to blue-green, seldom as markedly blue as in cultivated varieties. A spruce mainly of the s. Rockies.

WHITE SPRUCE *Picea glauca* (Moench) Voss
A pyramidal tree with twigs *hairless* (use lens after removing the needles). Needles yellow- to blue-green, *3/8"- 3/4"* long. Cones *cylindrical, 1 1/2"- 2"* in length with scales *smoothly rounded.* Cones *not* retained long on the tree. Height 50'- 60'; diameter 1'- 2'. Upland tundras and forests. Trees may live for 200 years. Crossbills and red squirrels consume the seeds; porcupines strip the inner bark; deer, moose, and bighorn sheep sometimes browse the twigs. In contrast to Black Spruce, White Spruce ranges southward over much of British Columbia to nw. Montana. Complete intergradation with Engelmann Spruce (Plate 6) occurs where ranges overlap and Engelmann Spruce is sometimes considered to be a subspecies of White Spruce.

BLACK SPRUCE *Picea mariana* (Mill.) BSP
Closely resembling White Spruce but with twigs *hairy* (use lens) and needles green to blue-green, only *1/4"- 7/16"* long. Cones ± *spherical, 3/4"- 1 1/4" long,* the scale tips *ragged.* Cones *tend to accumulate on the tree.* Height 25'- 30'; diameter 1'- 2'. Bogs and wet tundras. In British Columbia, Black Spruce extends southward mainly to central districts . `

PLATE 7

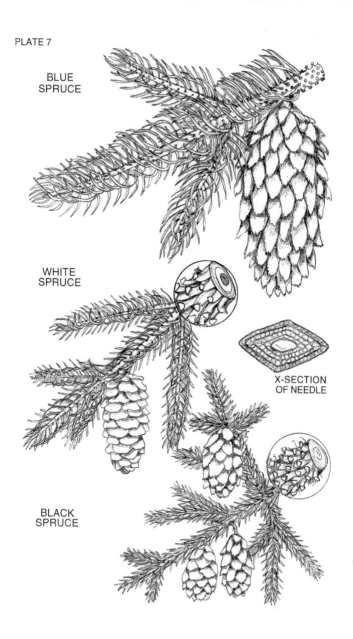

BLUE
SPRUCE

WHITE
SPRUCE

X-SECTION
OF NEEDLE

BLACK
SPRUCE

8. NEEDLES FLAT with TWIGS SHOWN: True Firs I

The Pacific Northwest displays one of the world's greatest concentrations of true firs (as distinct from Douglas-firs, Plate 12). True firs (genus *Abies*) are beautiful, steeple-shaped trees that thrive mainly in snowy climates.

Fir needles are single. PNW species have needles *blunt,* mainly with *double white-stripes* beneath. (Whitish markings on the needles of these and other conifers are lost from weathered or dried specimens; it is best to examine *fresh twig-end foliage.*) Buds are *rounded* and mostly *shiny* with resin. True firs resemble Douglas-firs in having smooth twigs with *circular* leaf scars. The trunk bark of young true firs is gray, mostly with resin-filled *blisters.* Older trunks are darker and usually furrowed. The topmost shoot is *erect.*

Fir cones are unique. They stand *upright* while ripening from green to purple. The scales are *thick and fleshy* but *soon fall,* leaving an erect but unobtrusive central stalk. Except in early summer, whole cones are seldom found unless cut down by squirrels before they mature. Bracts are mostly hidden between the cone scales (but see Noble Fir and a possible Red Fir hybrid, Plate 10).

In contrast to the firs of the following plates, these two species have needles *flat,* arranged *in flat sprays,* and with twigs *clearly visible* from above. Needles are mostly over 1/16" wide.

GRAND FIR *Abies grandis* (Dougl. ex Don) Lindl.
A handsome tree with needles *3/4"- 1"* (2") long, shiny, *dark-green,* and of *different lengths.* They are *white-lined* beneath, grooved above, and *notch-tipped* (use lens). Height 150'- 200' (250'); diameter 2'- 3' (5'). A fir of coastal regions from n. California to cen. British Columbia and also inland from cen. Oregon /cen. Idaho /nw. Montana to se. British Columbia. Fast-growing and tolerant of shade. The wood is reported to repel insects. May live nearly 300 years.

WHITE FIR *Abies concolor* (Gord. & Glend.) Hild.
A fir of low and middle elevations with needles in *flat sprays* ± curved upward in a *shallow U.* Needles *1 1/2"- 2 1/2" (3")* long, *pale blue-green,* dull, with two *pale green lines* beneath, tips *rounded,* and often *narrowed* at the base. Cones 3"- 5" long. Height 100'- 180' (210'); diameter 2'-5' (6'). Distributed from n. Mexico to cen. Oregon and se. Idaho. The specific name *concolor* refers to the uniform color of the needles. In Europe, plantings are often called Concolor Fir. The odorless wood was once in demand for butter tubs and cheese boxes. Intergrades with Grand Fir are reported. In coastal states, Sierra White Fir [*A. lowiana* (Gord.) A. Murray] has chemical distinctions as well as needle tips on the lower branches weakly notched (use lens).

PLATE 8

GRAND FIR

WHITE FIR

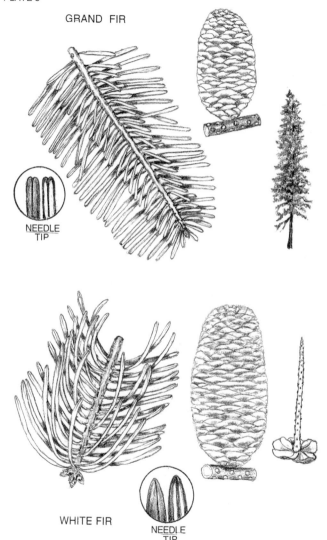

NEEDLE
TIP

NEEDLE
TIP

9. NEEDLES FLAT w/ TWIGS HIDDEN: True Firs II

Though with flat needles double-lined beneath like those of the trees on Plate 8, the foliage of these species appears to be in flat sprays only as viewed from *beneath*. For these firs and those of the next plate, many needles are J-shaped at the base. This curvature causes some needles to be directed upwards so as mostly to *hide* the twigs from above. In consequence, the twigs and their foliage tend to be fluffy and three-dimensional rather than in flat sprays. Cone bracts are hidden. Noble Fir (Plate 10) has needles flat with double white lines on both sides but only on the lower branches. Plate 8 reviews the group characteristics of true firs.

SILVER FIR *Abies amabilis* Dougl. ex J. Forbes
A beautiful fir with needles *1/2"- 1"* long, *dark green* above, *silvery-white* beneath, and *notched* at the tip (use lens). Mature cones purplish, 3 1/2"- 6" long. Twigs hairy or not. Trunk bark smoothish, gray. Height 75'- 100' (245'); diameter 2'- 4' (6'). A tree of foggy and rainy districts along the coast and on slopes of the Cascade Mountains from nw. California to extreme se. Alaska. Shallow-rooted and likely to be toppled by high winds. Blue and Spruce grouse eat the needles; Clark Nutcrackers and squirrels feed on the seeds. Often called "larch" by lumbermen, dating from times when firs were not much valued (see Plate 5). Also called Pacific Silver Fir.

SUBALPINE FIR *Abies lasiocarpa* (Hook.) Nutt.
A tree of cold climates and high elevations, from sea level in the far north to near timberline in the south. The narrow, *steeplelike* crown, though seen in other firs (and spruces) is typical. Needles 3/4"- 1 1/2" long and whitened *both above and beneath* with a *single white stripe above*. Needle tips rounded or notched. Twigs sometimes slightly hairy. Mature cones 2 1/2"- 4" long. Trunk bark grayish, smooth when young. Height 20'- 100' (130'); diameter 1'- 2' (7'). Ranges north from the Rocky Mountains of New Mexico /Arizona and the Cascade and Olympic mountains of Oregon /Washington to s. cen. Alaska and cen. Yukon. Often reproduces by layering where branches in contact with the ground take root, perhaps weighed down by snow. Formerly called Alpine Fir, but botanists now tend to restrict the term to tundra vegetation growing above timberline. Sometimes regarded as a form of *A. balsamea* (L.) Mill. of the East. Rocky Mountain trees are sometimes separated as Corkbark Fir (*A. bifolia* A. Murray) with magnified fresh leaf scar edges tan (not reddish) and basal bud scale edges smooth (not ragged).

PLATE 9

SILVER FIR

NEEDLE
TIP

X-SECTION
OF NEEDLE

SUBALPINE FIR

10. NEEDLES mostly 4-SIDED and TWIGS HIDDEN: True Firs III

Unlike the species of the previous two plates, the needles of these firs are ±*4-sided* (but see Noble Fir) and *easily twirled between the fingers.* They are blunt, whitened on *all* sides and, like those of the trees on Plate 9, twisted to *cover* the tops of twigs and branchlets. They are *not* in flat sprays. Some general characteristics of true firs are given on Plate 8.

NOBLE FIR *Abies procera* Rehd.

A tall tree with *slender* (under 1/16" wide), blue-green needles 1/2"- 1" long. Low branches mostly have *flat* needles with *double* white lines on *both* sides (use lens on fresh twig-end needles); needles on high (cone-bearing) branches mainly are *4-sided.* Twigs sometimes hairy (use lens); buds *dull* and *not* resinous. Cones 4"- 7" in length with distinctive long-pointed bracts that *fold downward,* nearly hiding the scales. Where cones are absent, cone scales and angled bracts often can be found nearby in piles left by squirrels. Trunk bark dark and rather smooth. Height 150'- 200' (275'); diameter 3'- 5' (9'). Mainly in the mountains of w. Oregon /w. Washington at 1500' -8000' elevations. Common at Crater Lake National Park, Oregon. In dense stands there may be few low branches. Once regarded as of poor quality (and hence sold as "larch", see Plate 5), it now has the highest value of any fir. Trees 600-700 years old have been found.

RED FIR *Abies magnifica* A. Murr.

An impressive forest tree mainly of the California Sierra Nevada. Needles 3/4"- 1 1/4" long, *all 4-sided, ridged* on top (use lens), whitened *above and below.* Twigs usually *hairy* (use lens). Cones 6"- 8" long, mostly brown-purple, the bracts *hidden* between the scales. Trunks reddish brown and deeply furrowed. Height 60'- 125' (175'); diameter 2'- 4' (8'), mainly at 5000'- 9000' elevations. Sooty grouse and pine grosbeaks eat the seeds. Though barely entering the PNW, a variety called Shasta Red Fir (var. *shastensis* Lemmon) extends from n. California to the Cascades of s. Oregon. It has cones with visible angled bracts and may be a Red Fir-Noble Fir hybrid.

PLATE 10

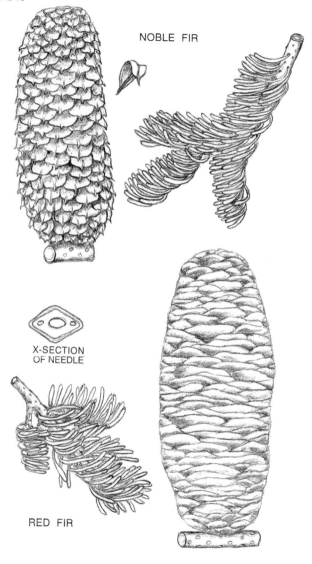

NOBLE FIR

X-SECTION
OF NEEDLE

RED FIR

11. NEEDLES FLAT following along TWIGS:
Pacific Yew and Redwood

Resembling the firs of Plate 8 and the first two species of Plate 12, the conifers of this plate have *flat* needles arranged in *flat sprays* (but see Redwood). Further, like some species of Plate 12, Pacific Yew has thin hairlike needle stalks and Redwood has white-striped needles at least on the lower branches.

The needle bases of both of these species are extended to *follow along the twigs.* Twigs are *green.* The leader shoots do *not* droop. The fruits of yews are unlike those of other conifers in being *fleshy, red,* and *open-ended.*

PACIFIC YEW *Taxus brevifolia* Nutt.
    An often shrubby species with needles 1/2"- 1" long, *stalked,* and *green* on both sides. Twigs *green;* buds brown, hairless, and *pointed.* Mature fruits (on female trees) *bright red,* juicy, with an open end revealing a dark seed. Trunk bark thin and peeling. Height 25'- 50' (75'); diameter 1'- 2' (4'). Forests to 7000' elevation on the Pacific slope from n. California to se. Alaska and also in the ne. Washington /n. Idaho /s. British Columbia region. Mature foliage may be poisonous to livestock. Yew wood was valued by Native Americans for making bows. The drug *taxol,* first obtained from this plant, has proven to be helpful in the treatment of some cancers.

REDWOOD *Sequoia sempervirens* (D. Don.) Endl.
    This, the tallest and probably the most impressively beautiful tree in North America, barely enters the Pacific Northwest in sw. Oregon. Needles on low branches are *flat,* mostly 1/2"- 1 1/4" long, *white-lined* beneath, and *not* stalked. Needles on high branches and at some twig ends, however, may be slim, *awl-shaped,* and only 1/4"- 1/2" long. These short, sharp needles are *not* in flat sprays. Buds are *blunt.* Cones are 3/4"- 1" long, brown, woody, and *thick-scaled.* Trunks are often buttressed at the base. The trunk bark is red-brown, fibrous, and often a foot thick. Sprouts are frequent, especially at the trunk base. Height 150'- 350' (365'); diameter 10'- 18' (33'). The groves of straight and immensely tall specimens along the narrow belt of coastal fogs in n. California and sw. Oregon are world renowned. Bottomlands and moist soils.

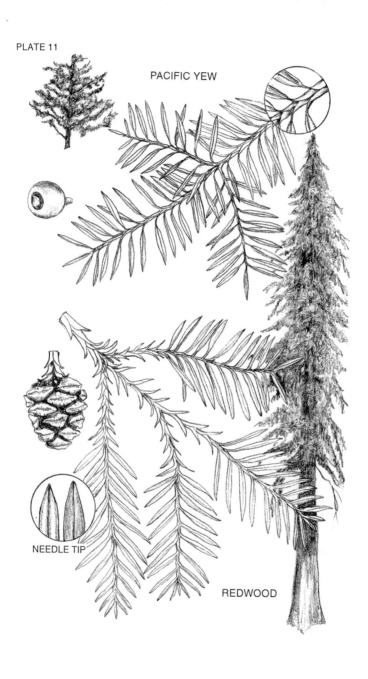

PLATE 11

PACIFIC YEW

NEEDLE TIP

REDWOOD

12. NEEDLES ± FLAT on THIN STALKS

The needles of these trees are attached to the twigs by almost-hairlike *thin stalks* (see also Pacific Yew, Plate 11). They are *white-banded* beneath (see also Plates 8-11) and, except for Mountain Hemlock, are *flat* and in *flat sprays*. (Note: whitish markings on the needles of these and other conifers disappear from weathered or dried specimens; it is best to examine *fresh twig-end foliage*.) Cones are dry, brown, *pendent,* and do not shed their scales.

Hemlocks often can be recognized even at a considerable distance by the 1'- 3' long top leader shoot which has a characteristic *droop* (see also Deodar Cedar, Plate 5, and native "cedars", Plate 13).

COMMON DOUGLAS-FIR *Pseudotsuga menziesii* (Mirb.) Franco
  Best field marks are twigs that *droop* markedly and *3-pointed bracts* that protrude from between the woody cone scales (cones usually many beneath the tree). Needles 3/4"- 1 1/2" long. As in true firs, plucked twigs show *smooth circular* leaf scars. Buds, however, are sharply *pointed.* The topmost shoot stands *erect.* Trunk bark dark and grooved. Height 80'- 100' (300'); diameter 2'- 5' (14'). An important lumber tree common throughout western mountains, north nearly to se. Alaska. Named for David Douglas, an early Scottish botanist, but found by Archibald Menzies one of Douglas' countrymen. *Pseudotsuga* means false-hemlock, possibly a good common name. Bigcone Douglas-fir [P. *macrocarpa* (Vasey) Mayr] occurs in sw. Calif.

WESTERN HEMLOCK *Tsuga heterophylla* (Raf.) Sarg.
  An attractive tree with needles only 1/4"- 3/4" long and of *different lengths.* They are attached to *weak* woody pegs that make dead twigs *slightly* rough (see spruces, Plate 6). Cones delicate, only 3/4"- 1" long. Trunk brown to gray with scaly ridges. Height 125'- 160' (200'); diameter 2'- 5' (10'). At low to middle elevations on Pacific slopes from n. California to s. Alaska and again in the Rocky Mountains of ne. Washington /n. Idaho /nw. Montana to se. British Columbia /sw. Alberta. Hemlocks are more shade-tolerant than most conifers. Native Americans made flour from the inner bark in emergencies.

MOUNTAIN HEMLOCK *Tsuga mertensiana* (Bong.) Carr.
  A coastal and inland tree of high elevations and other areas of deep snow. Needles are on *weak* pegs, only 1/4"- 3/4" long, *± rounded* in cross-section, and *spreading starlike in all directions. All* surfaces are whitened, the tree appearing ± blue-green. Cones 1 1/2"-2" (3") long, brown, narrow. Height 30'- 100' (150'); diameter 1'- 3' (6'). Found from the Sierra Nevada /Cascades to s. Alaska and in the n. Idaho /se. British Columbia region of the Rocky Mountains.

PLATE 12

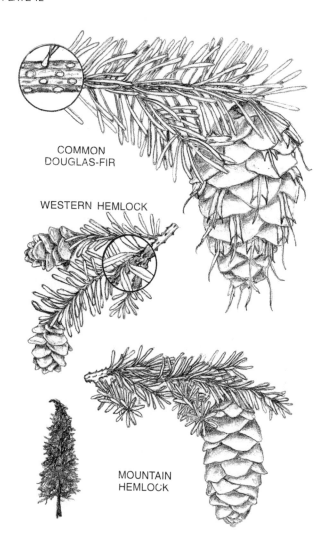

COMMON
DOUGLAS-FIR

WESTERN HEMLOCK

MOUNTAIN
HEMLOCK

13. LEAVES SCALELIKE in FLAT SPRAYS

These are characteristic trees of the PNW and some of the most magnificent on the continent. Though called "cedars", none is a true *Cedrus* (see Plate 5). Twigs are densely covered by small, *scalelike*, mostly aromatic leaves arranged in *flat sprays* (photos p. 54). Gland dots mostly absent. Cones *brown-woody* when mature. Leader shoot short, but may droop or lean (see hemlocks Plate 12).

WESTERN REDCEDAR *Thuja plicata* Donn ex D. Don

A beautiful and commercially valuable tree also called Western Arborvitae. Leaves pale green, 1/16"- 1/8" long, mostly *whitened* beneath in a so-called butterfly pattern (use lens), and edges *smoothly rounded*. Foliage *droops*, forming inverted Vs at branch ends. Cones *slender, 1/2"- 3/4" long, upright,* with *8-10* scales, mostly clustered. Trunks red-brown, *vertically grooved,* often with basal buttresses. Height 60'- 130' (180'); diameter 1'- 2' (20'). From nw. California to se. Alaska and also in the Rockies from e. Washington /nw. Montana to cen. British Columbia. Lumber strong, durable. Native Americans made the trunks into war canoes holding 40 people. Ropes, nets, blankets, baskets, and roof thatch also were made from the fibrous bark.

ALASKA-CEDAR *Chamaecyparis nootkatensis* (D. Don) Sudw.

Resembles Western Redcedar but leaf scales are *without* white markings and have *pointed* tips directed *outward* (use lens). Foliage sprays mostly *hang vertically.* Cones *spherical, 3/8"- 1/2"* wide, the *4-6* scales with central *points.* Inner bark *yellow.* Mature trunk bark *flaky.* Height 50'- 100' (150'); diameter 1'- 3' (10'). Also called Yellow-cedar. A valuable species, thriving along foggy coasts from extreme nw. California to s. Alaska. First found at Nootka, Vancouver Island.

PORT ORFORD-CEDAR *Chamaecyparis lawsoniana* (A. Murr.) Parl.

Planted worldwide in many horticultural forms. Foliage *not* drooping; leaves ± 1/16' long, with thin, white, *x-marks* beneath (use lens), and *glands* present. Cones round, 1/4"- 3/8" wide, with *7-10 smooth* scales. Height 110'- 175' (200'); diameter 1'- 3' (6'). Native in nw. California and sw. Oregon. Also called Lawson-cedar.

INCENSE-CEDAR *Calocedrus decurrens* (Torr.) Florin

A beautiful large, cone-shaped tree with *long* (to 1/2"), *glossy* foliage scales in unique *vase-shaped whorls* (use lens). Gland dots *lacking.* Cones 3/4"- 1" long, *pendent,* with six brown scales, two of them quite short. Trunk bark red-brown, furrowed. Height 60'- 80' (100'); diameter 3'- 4' (7'). Middle elevations, from nw. Mexico to nw. Oregon, local in cen. Oregon. Wood fragrant and durable, used to make cedar chests, shingles, and pencils. Related species grow in Chile, China, and the South Pacific. Formerly in the genus *Libocedrus.*

PLATE 13

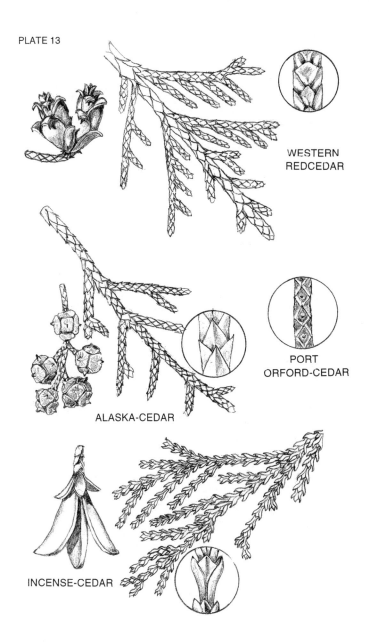

WESTERN
REDCEDAR

ALASKA-CEDAR

PORT
ORFORD-CEDAR

INCENSE-CEDAR

14. SCALELIKE LEAVES NOT in FLAT SPRAYS

Both **junipers** and **cypresses** have blunt leaf scales under 1/4"
long, mostly *gland-dotted* (use lens), and frequently aromatic.
These scales hug twigs that are often 4-sided and mostly *not* in flat
sprays. Junipers tend to have small, sharp, awl-shaped needles
present *in addition to* leaf scales; cypresses have *only* scalelike
leaves. Juniper fruits (essentially cones with fused scales) are
mostly 1/4"- 1/2" wide, ± spherical, blue or red-brown when
mature, and *hard-fleshy,* usually with a whitish powder. The sexes
are separate in some junipers, hence male trees *lack* fruits. Juniper
berries, too, tend to fall when mature (in 1-2 years) and also
disappear when eaten by wildlife. Cypresses, on the other hand,
have both sexes on the *same* tree and produce *woody, brown,* ball-
shaped, inedible cones usually *present* on the tree being examined.

JUNIPERS *Juniperus* species

Trunk bark generally red-brown and shreddy. When dried, bark
rubbed between the hands is good for starting fires. Native
Americans and settlers ate juniper berries raw or ground into
flour, perhaps mixed with other foods. Many wildlife species
also consume the fruits. Most junipers occur on dry slopes.

Rocky Mountain Juniper (*J. scopulorum* Sarg.) has scaly
twigs thin, *threadlike* [only about 1/32" thick], ± 4-sided, and
drooping. Leaf scales bluish- to *dark* green and ± *long-pointed.*
Mature fruits bright *blue,* juicy. Height 15'- 30 (40'); diameter
1'- 2' (9'). Found from Arizona and w. Texas to ne. Oregon,
nw. Washingon, se. British Columbia, and sw. Alberta.
Western (Sierra) Juniper (*J. occidentalis* Hook.) has wider
(± 1/16") twigs, leaf scales *gray*-green, and *not* long-pointed.
Fruits *blue-black,* juicy. Height 10'- 25' (85'); diameter 2'- 3'
(15'). From s. California to sw. Idaho and cen. Washington.
Extensive stands occur in e. Oregon. **Utah Juniper**
[*J. osteosperma* (Torr.) Little] has leaf scales *yellow*-green,
short-pointed, and *lacking* glands. Mature fruits are *red-brown*
and *dry.* Height 15'-20' (40'); diameter 8"- 12" (36").
Southwestern states, reaching our region in se. Idaho.

BAKER CYPRESS *Cupressus bakeri* Jeps.

A tree whose *very slender,* 4-sided twigs are covered with gray-
to dark-green, *long-pointed* scales only ± 1/16" long. Cones
mostly *6-scaled, warty,* and 3/8"- 3/4" in diameter. Trunk bark
tight, gray. Height 30'- 50' (80'); diameter 1'- 2'. Local,
n. California to Josephine and Jackson Counties in sw. Oregon.
Milo Baker, a California botanist, found the species in the 19th
century. Also called Modoc or Matthew Cypress.

PLATE 14

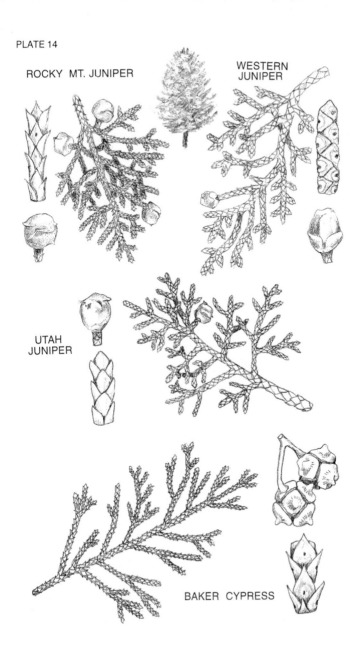

ROCKY MT. JUNIPER

WESTERN JUNIPER

UTAH JUNIPER

BAKER CYPRESS

II. Trees with Opposite Compound Leaves

In contrast to the needleleaf species of Plates 1-14, all other trees in the Pacific Northwest are *broadleaf* plants with either compound or simple foliage. Only ten regional tree species have *compound* leaves. The four on this plate and the next have *opposite* foliage while the six on Plates 21-22 have *alternate* leaves. When leaves have fallen, the bare twigs of all opposite-leaved species (Plates 15-20) may need to be compared. *Be sure not to mistake the leaflets of a compound leaf for the blades of simple leaves* (see Figure 1, page 10).

15. LEAVES FEATHER-COMPOUND:
Oregon Ash and Ashleaf Maple

The species of Plates 15-16 have feather-compound leaves arranged in opposing pairs and mostly toothed. The twigs, too, are mostly oppositely branched. Unlike the species of Plate 16, the trees of this plate have leaflet bases *even*, pith *narrow*, and the central end bud *present.* The opposite leaves of Western Mountain Maple (Plate 17) also sometimes may be trifoliate-compound.

OREGON ASH *Fraxinus latifolia* Benth.

Often a large tree with leaves *5"- 12"* long and leaflets 5-7 per leaf. Each leaflet 3"- 5" long, mostly *not* stalked, somewhat *hairy* beneath, often *wavy-edged* or slightly toothed. Buds *brown,* rounded, with a *smooth, grainy* appearance. Leaf scars *shield-shaped,* with *many* bundle scars, and *no* connecting lines between them. Flowers small, dark, clustered, *without* petals, in early spring usually ahead of the leaves. Fruits 1"- 2" long, the wing resembling the blade of a tiny canoe-paddle. Mature trunk dark gray with a close network of fine fissures. Height to 80'; diameter to 4'. Floodplains, mainly west of the Cascades from s. California to sw. British Columbia. Wood valued for baseball bats and canoe paddles. **European Ash** (*F. excelsior* L.), often planted, has *7-13* leaflets *not* toothed and *black* buds.

ASHLEAF MAPLE (BOX-ELDER) *Acer negundo* L.

A maple with opposite compound leaves. The 3 (-5) leaflets are 2"- 5" long with several *large jagged* teeth. Twigs *stout, green* or purplish; buds white-hairy; the opposite leaf scars meeting in *raised points.* Bundle scars *3 (-5).* Fruits, like those of all maples, are *paired winged* "keys". Height 50'- 75', diameter 1'- 2'. Naturalized in Oregon /Washington /sw. B. C., growing mainly in bottomlands. While box-elder is the more-common name and the weak wood is used for boxes, the tree is not closely related to elderberries. Ashleaf Maple is emphasized here in a small effort to popularize a perhaps more-suitable name. Trifoliate leaves resemble those of Poison-oak [*Toxicodendron diversilobium* (Torrey & Gray) Greene] but that shrubby non-oak has alternate leaves.

PLATE 15

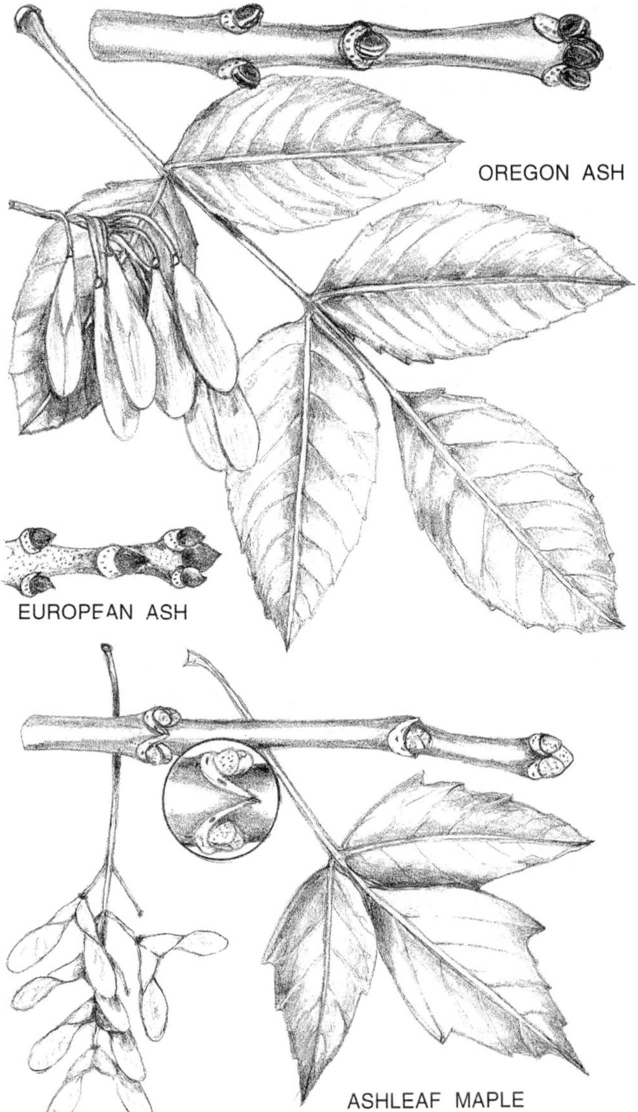

OREGON ASH

EUROPEAN ASH

ASHLEAF MAPLE

16. LEAVES FEATHER-COMPOUND : Elderberries

Unlike Oregon Ash and Ashleaf Maple (Plate 15), elderberries are shrubs or small trees whose toothed leaflets mostly have *uneven* bases and whose *weak* twigs contain *wide* pith. Buds are obviously *scaly*, *lines* connect the paired leaf scars, and a central end bud is *lacking*. Bundle scars are 5 (3-7). The tiny, white flowers and *juicy, several-seeded* fruits occur in conspicuous end clusters. Fruits must be cooked but are sometimes made into jams, jellies, and pies. Toy whistles and flutes can be made from the hollowed twigs.

These two species have leaflets variably 2"- 6" long and short- to long-pointed

BLUE ELDERBERRY *Sambucus mexicana* C. Presl
A widespread western elderberry. Leaves 5"- 8" long with *5-9 hairless* and mostly *fine-toothed* leaflets. Pith *white* or brown. Flower clusters 2"- 8" across, *flat-topped,* June-Sept.; fruits dark but white-powdered, a beautiful *sky-blue* color. Though mostly shrubby, some plants become 25' tall. On open sites from Baja California and w. Texas north to s. British Columbia. Also called *S. caerulea* Raf.

RED ELDERBERRY *Sambucus racemosa* L.
A coastal species with leaves 4"- 11" long bearing *5-7 fine-toothed* leaflets often *hairy* beneath. Pith *brown,* sometimes pale. Flowers March-July; fruits *bright red,* in *cone-shaped* clusters 3"- 4" wide, June-Oct. Height to 32'. Forest edges. Coastal regions from n. California to s. Alaska. Also called Pacific Red Elderberry and Redberry Elder. An earlier scientific name was *S. callicarpa* Greene. A shrubby elderberry also with cone-shaped flower /fruit clusters and red berries occurs at relatively high elevations throughout the West. It is listed in Hickman (1993) as the more or less hairless var. *microbotrys* (Rydb.) Kearney & Peebles.

PLATE 16

BLUE
ELDERBERRY

RED
ELDERBERRY

III. Trees with Opposite Simple Leaves

Trees of this type are shown on this plate and the next three. When leafless, compare also with Plates 15-16.

17. LEAVES FAN-LOBED : Native Maples

The only trees with opposite fan-lobed foliage in the PNW are maples, and only they have the *paired, dry, winged* fruits called *keys*. The leafstalks of maples are *long*, with sap mostly *clear*. Bundle scars are *three*. Autumn foliage is colorful and the springtime sap can be boiled into syrup. Ashleaf Maple (Box Elder), with compound leaves, is on Plate 15. Some maples introduced from other areas are reviewed on Plate 18. English Hawthorn (Plate 23) and White Poplar (Plate 25) may have some maplelike leaves but they are alternate.

BIGLEAF MAPLE *Acer macrophyllum* Pursh

A maple with *very* large leaves. Leaves *16"- 24"* long including the 8"- 12" stalks. Leaf lobes *5*, each with several *rounded* teeth. Leafstalk sap *milky*, usually best seen when the leafstalk base is pulled from the twig. Twigs *stout*, buds *many-scaled, blunt*. Flower clusters *slender*, drooping, 4"-6" long, April-May. Single fruit *1 1/2"- 2"* long, paired keys form a *narrow V*, May-July. Height to 100'; diameter to 3'- 5' (8'). On the Pacific slope from s. California to cen. British Columbia, also in the Sierra Nevada. Lumber used for panels and furniture. Fertile soils to 5000' elevation.

WESTERN MOUNTAIN MAPLE *Acer glabrum* Pursh.

This shrub or small tree has leaves *4"- 7"* long, *3-5* lobed, and leaf teeth *sharp*. Foliage sometimes is divided into *three coarse-toothed leaflets* (see Plate 15). Twigs *red-brown*; buds *sharp*, with only *two* scales. Flowers in *umbrella-shaped* groups, May-July. Single fruit *3/4"- 1"* long, paired fruits in a *wide V*, August-September. Trees sometimes attain a height of 40' and a diameter of 15". Found from the Sierra Nevada and s. Rockies to se. Alaska. Also known as Rocky Mountain Maple or Douglas Maple. In winter, dogwoods (Plate 18) also show two bud scales but fruits are fleshy and twig leaf scars are raised.

VINE MAPLE *Acer circinatum* Pursh

A tree of the PNW's Pacific slope. Leaves *7-9* lobed, *3"- 6"* long, *sharply* toothed, and almost *circular*. Twigs *slender*, green or purplish; buds *blunt*, with 2-4 scales. Flower clusters *rounded*, spring. Single fruit *1/2"- 3/4"* long, paired keys forming a nearly *straight line*. Height sometimes to 40', a weak and reclining stem often preventing the plant from reaching tree height. Damp forests to 5000' elevation from n. California to sw. British Columbia.

CANYON MAPLE, in sw. Montana /se. Idaho see p. 48

PLATE 17

BIGLEAF MAPLE

WESTERN
MOUNTAIN MAPLE

VINE
MAPLE

18. LEAVES FAN-LOBED: Introduced Maples

Maples imported from other areas are frequently seen in parks and along streets in parts of the Pacific Northwest. Occasionally, they spread from plantings. Those on this plate are among the more frequently encountered kinds. Leaves are mostly 4"- 9" long. Leafstalk sap is *clear,* except in Norway Maple. Buds are many-scaled. Flower /fruit clusters are *short* and *rounded,* except in Sycamore Maple. The general characteristics of maples, are given on Plate 17.

Red and Silver maples, imported from the eastern United States, have foliage *whitened* beneath and buds *red:*

RED MAPLE *Acer rubrum* L.
Foliage *3-5 lobed,* the spaces between the leaf lobes shallowly *V-shaped.* A single fruit is *1/2"- 1"* long.

SILVER MAPLE *Acer saccharinum* L.
Leaves *5-lobed,* the spaces between the leaf lobes deeply *U-shaped.* A single fruit is *1 1/2"- 3"* long.

Norway and Sycamore maples are of European origin. Their leaf undersides and buds are both *green:*

NORWAY MAPLE *Acer platanoides* L.
Foliage *5-7 lobed,* leaf teeth *sharp.* A single fruit is *1 1/2"* long. The leafstalk yields a *milky* sap.

SYCAMORE MAPLE *Acer pseudoplatanus* L.
Leaves of Sycamore Maple are *5-lobed,* the leaf teeth are *rounded,* and single fruits are *2"- 4"* long. The leafstalk sap is *clear* and flower clusters are *long* and *slender.*

CANYON MAPLE *Acer grandidentatum* Nutt. (from p. 46)
A small-foliaged maple with leaves *2"- 4 1/2"* long and equally wide. Leaf teeth *rounded,* large, relatively *few,* and widely-spaced. Buds mostly *4-scaled.* Flowers April-May. Single fruit 1/2"- 1" long, in U-shaped pairs, June-September. A tree of the Rocky Mountains, ranging from s. cen. Montana and se. Idaho to Mexico. Also known as Bigtooth Maple, a translation of the scientific name. Sometimes tapped for its sweet sap and called Sugar Maple, though that name is better reserved for the eastern *A. saccharum* that yields the maple sugar and maple syrup of commerce (two of the few foods native to North America).

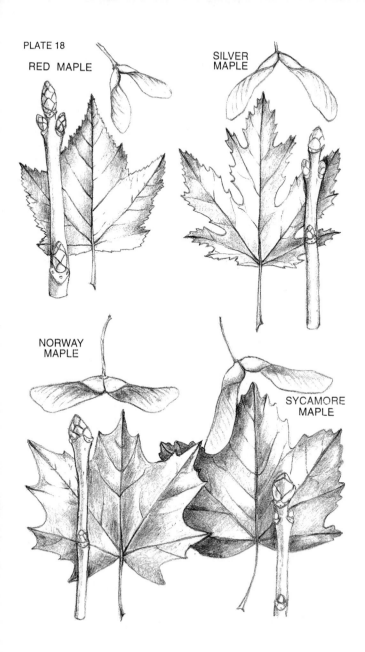

PLATE 18

RED MAPLE

SILVER MAPLE

NORWAY MAPLE

SYCAMORE MAPLE

19. VEINS FOLLOW LEAF EDGES: Dogwoods

Dogwoods have leaves *not* lobed, mostly *without* teeth, and with lateral leaf veins that *tend to follow the leaf edges.* Leaves ± egg-shaped, short-pointed, mostly with 4-7 vein pairs. Twigs dark (red in one species) with either *brown or white* pith. Buds with only *two* scales and bundle scars *three* per leaf scar. Flowers small, mostly white, appearing after the leaves - but see Pacific Dogwood. Fruits small, fleshy, mostly *stalked,* and 1-2 seeded. Twigs browsed by deer, elk, moose, cottontail rabbits, and snowshoe hares; fruits eaten by ruffed and sharptail grouse, bandtail pigeons, and other birds.

PACIFIC DOGWOOD *Cornus nuttallii* Audubon
  A small to large tree well known for its showy springtime blossoms.The flowers, small and crowded into tight heads, are circled by 4-6 mostly *pointed white bracts* each 2"-3" long. Leaves *3"- 5"* long, sometimes almost circular, ± hairy beneath, and with *4-6* pairs of side veins. Foliage occasionally fine-toothed or wavy-edged, unlike other dogwoods. Twig pith *brown.* Flowers appear *before* or with the leaves, March-May; fruits *without* stalks, *red or orange,* in clusters of 20-40, September-November. Height to 100'; diameter to 2'. Ranges north along the Pacific slope to sw. British Columbia, also in the Sierra Nevada. Native Americans are said to have boiled the bark to make a laxative drink. **Flowering Dogwood** (*C. florida* L.) of e. North America, often planted in parks, has *white* pith, four *square-ended* flower bracts, and *4 (-8)* red fruits per cluster.

SMOOTH (BROWN) DOGWOOD *Cornus glabrata* Benth.
  A small tree or shrub also with *brown* pith but whose leaves are only *1"- 2 1/2"* long, *hairless,* with *3-4* pairs of lateral veins. Twigs brown to red-purple, often *drooping.* Flowers May-June; fruits *white,* Aug.-Sept. Height to 20'. Moist soils below 5000' elevation. Coastal mountains, s. California to sw. Oregon.

WESTERN DOGWOOD
  Cornus sericea L. ssp. *occidentalis* (Torr. & Gray) Cov.
  A small tree with foliage like that of Pacific Dogwood but *densely* hairy beneath. Twigs red-purple, *hairy;* pith *whitish* to tan. Fruits *white,* with a *grooved* stone. Height to 15'. Coastal slopes to 8000' elevation, from s. California to nw. Washington. This and the next subspecies called American Dogwood in Hickman (1993). Earlier named *C. occidentalis.*

RED-OSIER DOGWOOD *Cornus sericea* L. ssp. *sericea*
  Widespread over much of US /Canada north to cen. Alaska and sw. Yukon. Twigs *bright red* (sometimes green) and pith *white.* Leaves 2"-4" long, ± hairy, with *4-7* pairs of side veins. Flowers May-July; fruits *white,* stone smooth, July-December. To 26' tall. Moist sites. Previously named *C. stolonifera.*

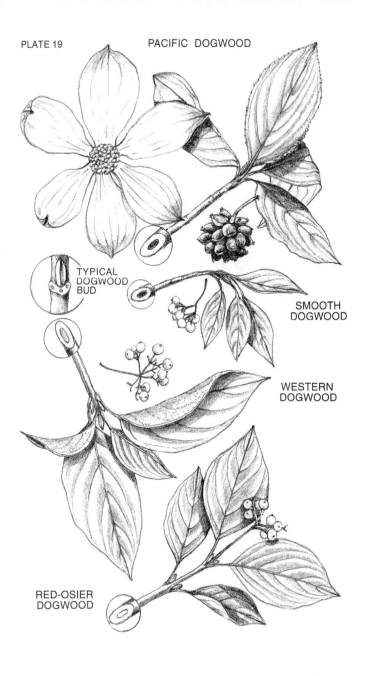

PLATE 19

PACIFIC DOGWOOD

TYPICAL
DOGWOOD
BUD

SMOOTH
DOGWOOD

WESTERN
DOGWOOD

RED-OSIER
DOGWOOD

20. OPPOSITE LEAVES either SILVERY, TOOTHED, or WAVY-EDGED

The first two species are deciduous, the third is the only opposite-leaved *evergreen* tree in the region. Pacific Dogwood (Plate 19), may have some leaves fine-toothed or wavy-edged. Cascara and California buckthorns (Plates 38, 39) may have fine-toothed leaves sometimes opposite.

SILVER BUFFALOBERRY *Shepherdia argentea* Nutt.
A native woody plant with *silver-scaly* foliage, twigs, and buds. Leaves *smooth-edged, 1"- 2 1/2"* long, more or less leathery, with bases *V-shaped*. Additional small leaves may be present at the leafstalk bases. Twigs frequently *thorn-tipped*; bud scales *two;* bundle scar *one*. Flowers small, greenish, lacking petals, April-June; fruits small, orange-red, fleshy, July-Sept. To 15' in height. West across the plains to e. cen. Idaho, nw. Montana, ne. Washington, se. British Columbia, and se. Alberta. Also in the Southwest, extending north to se. Oregon. The fruits reportedly can be made into jelly. Russian-olive (Plate 32), a widely-planted and ± thorny imported tree, also has silver-scaly foliage and twigs but its leaves are alternate.

WESTERN BURNINGBUSH *Euonymus occidentalis* Torr.
A shrub or small tree with leaves 2"- 4" long, *fine-toothed,* hairless, and pointed at *both* ends. Twigs *green* and 4-angled or *4-lined*. Bud scales *several;* bundle scar *one*. Flowers long-stemmed, purplish, April-June; fruits red, fleshy, beneath wide, dry, 3-5-parted bracts. To 20' tall. Canyons and slopes to 6000' elevation in coast ranges north to sw. Washingon, local sw. British Columbia.

WAVYLEAF SILKTASSEL *Garrya elliptica* Lindl.
A small tree or shrub whose thick, *evergreen* leaves are 3"- 5" long, *woolly* beneath, with *U-shaped* bases, and strongly *undulant* edges. Twigs *gray-brown,* 4-angled or *4-lined*, bud scales *2-4,* and bundle scars *three*. Flowers small, in drooping catkins 3"- 6" long, January-March; fruits small, dry, densely white-hairy, June-August. Height to 20'. Found below 2000' elevation on coastal slopes from Oregon southward. Nicholas Garry was an early 19th-century official of the Hudson's Bay Company and a friend of David Douglas for whom Douglas-fir was named.

PLATE 20

SILVER BUFFALOBERRY

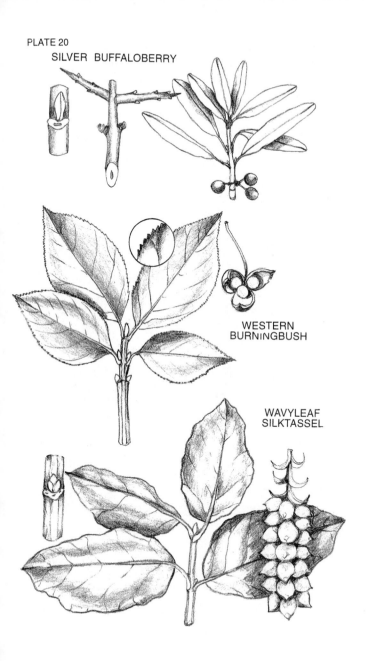

WESTERN
BURNINGBUSH

WAVYLEAF
SILKTASSEL

"Cedars"
Plate 13

Western
Redcedar
- fronds and
mature cones

Alaska-
cedar
- green
cones
(within
fronds)

Incense-cedar
- fronds and
mature cones

Some Trees with Distinctive Bark

Western White Pine - Plate 1

Netleaf Hackberry - Plate 24

Whiteleaf Manzanita - Plate 40

Red Alder - Plate 34

IV. Trees with Alternate Compound Leaves

The trees of Plates 21-22 have alternate feather-compound foliage (trees with fan-compound leaves grow wild in other regions) and 7 to 41 mostly *narrow, toothed* leaflets. On Plate 22, however, Tree-of-Heaven has only a few teeth and Block Locust is *thorny* with mainly *toothless* leaflets. *Do not mistake the leaflets of a compound leaf for the blades of simple leaves.*

21. MOUNTAIN-ASHES

Mountain-ashes are cold-hardy trees with more or less flat-topped clusters of small, white blossoms and *applelike* fruits $1/4"-1/2"$ in diameter. Leaves are *4"-9"* long with *7-15* leaflets, twigs are *slender* with *narrow* pith, leaf scars are *narrowly crescent-shaped* with *five* bundle scars, spur branches are usually *present*. Trunk bark is gray and smooth in the first two species. Sharptail and ruffed grouse, ptarmigan, martens, and fishers all eat the fruits, as do some people. Much used in landscaping. Some species grow as far north as Alaska, Labrador, Greenland, Iceland, and n. Europe*. Oregon ash (Plate 15) has opposite, feather-compound leaves.

SITKA MOUNTAIN-ASH *Sorbus sitchensis* Roem.
The leaves of this small tree have 7-11 *blunt-tipped* leaflets with the basal $1/3-1/2$ of the leaf edges *not* toothed. Twigs and winter buds *rusty-hairy*. Flowers around $1/4"$ wide, the clusters *2"-4"* in diameter, June to August; fruits *orange* to red, nearly $1/2"$ across, August to winter. Forest openings, cen. California, se. Oregon, and nw. Montana to sw. Alaska and sw. Yukon. First discovered near Sitka, se. Alaska.

GREENE MOUNTAIN-ASH *Sorbus scopulina* E. Greene
Often shrubby with leaflets *fully toothed, long-pointed*, and 11-15 per leaf. Twigs and buds more or less *hairless*. Flowers around $3/8"$ in diameter, in clusters *1"-3"* across, August to September; fruits *red*, $1/4"-3/8"$ wide, July to August. Height to 20'. From California and New Mexico to sw. Alaska and s. Yukon. Botanist Edward L. Greene named the species. Also called Western Mountain-ash.

EUROPEAN MOUNTAIN-ASH *Sorbus aucuparia* L.
Introduced into the East during colonial days and now growing wild in scattered locations across the continent. Leaflets 9-15, *short-pointed*, often *white-hairy* beneath, and toothed *nearly* to the base. Twigs hairless; buds *white-hairy*. Trunk with *horizontal streaks*. Flowers $3/8"$ wide, the clusters *4"-6"* in diameter, May to June; fruits *red*, $5/16"-3/8"$ in diameter, August to October or later. Height to 40'; diameter 6" to 12". The species' name refers to the traditional use of the sticky sap to catch birds. Reportedly, the only exotic tree to grow wild in Alaska.

*In Europe, often called servicetree, possibly a corruption of Sorbustree and perhaps the basis for the name of our serviceberry (Plate 38).

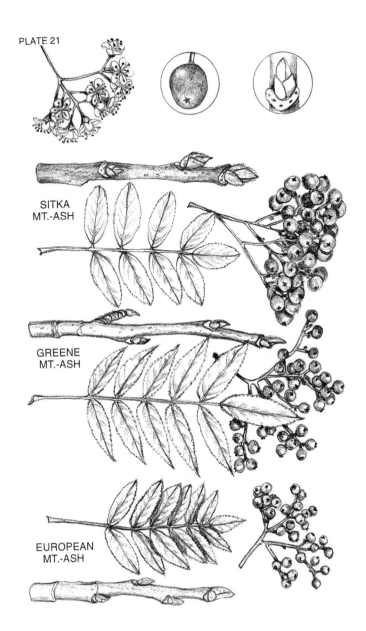

PLATE 21

SITKA
MT.-ASH

GREENE
MT.-ASH

EUROPEAN
MT.-ASH

22. Smooth Sumac, Tree-of-Heaven, Black Locust

Like the mountain-ashes of Plate 21, **Smooth Sumac and Tree-of-Heaven** have compound foliage with leaflets narrow. These species differ, however, in that leaves are *12"-24"* long, leaflets are *11-41* per leaf, twigs are *thick,* pith is *wide,* bundle scars are *many* per leaf scar, and spur branches are *lacking.* The trunk bark is brown, often smooth, and not distinctive.

SMOOTH SUMAC *Rhus glabra* L.
A small tree whose leaves have 11-31 long-pointed and *coarse-toothed* leaflets. Twigs ± *flat-sided;* buds *white-hairy;* leaf scars *U-shaped.* Flowers small, greenish, in upright groups, June-July; fruits each 1/8" long, dry, *red-hairy,* tightly clustered, July-winter. Height 4'- 10' (25'); diameter 1"- 3" (6"). A mostly-eastern tree found locally on sunny sites from n. Oregon and cen. Idaho to s. British Columbia. A "lemonade" can be made from the fruits. Raw sprouts are reported to have been eaten by Native Americans. Twigs are browsed by rabbits and deer while sharptail and ruffed grouse, ringneck pheasants, mourning doves, and many songbirds sometimes consume the fruits.

TREE-OF-HEAVEN *Ailanthus altissima* (Mill.) Swingle
An Oriental tree fast-growing on disturbed sites. Leaves 1'- 2' long with 11-41 leaflets that lack teeth *except for 1-2 gland-tipped pairs near the leaf base.* Buds *brown-hairy;* leaf scars *very large, triangular.* Flowers clustered, yellowish, June-July; fruits 1"- 2" long, one-seeded, papery, winged, often in large groups, September-winter. Height to 80'- 100'; diameter to 1'- 2'. Occurs north to s. British Columbia. Immune to dust and smoke. May grow 8' or more a year; sprouts 12' long are not uncommon. The common name, probably of Asiatic origin, may allude to the tree's height.

Black Locust is the region's only wild tree with paired thorns and its only thorny tree with compound leaves. Though native to eastern North America, it is spreading rapidly in temperate zones around the world. In the PNW, it occurs north to s. British Columbia.

BLACK LOCUST *Robinia pseudoacacia* L.
Leaves 8"- 14" long, the 7-19 leaflets *blunt-tipped* and mostly *without* teeth. Buds *break through* the leaf scars *flanked* by thorns. Flowers white, pealike, in drooping clusters 4"- 6" long, spring; fruits flat, dry, *pods* 2"- 6" in length. Trunk dark with distinctive thick, intersecting ridges. Height 70'- 100'; diameter 2'- 4'. Wood makes durable fence posts. Seeds and bark listed as poisonous to humans and livestock.

PLATE 22

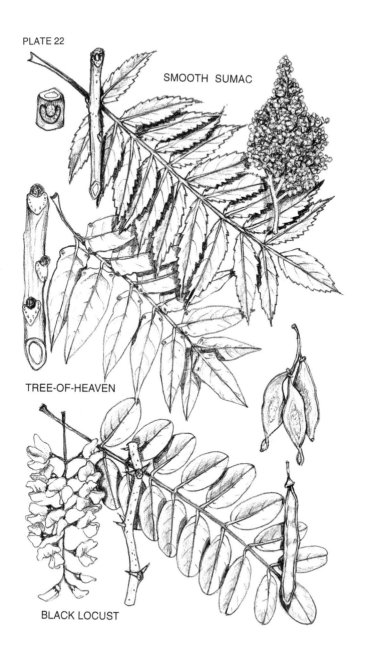

SMOOTH SUMAC

TREE-OF-HEAVEN

BLACK LOCUST

V. TREES w/ ALTERNATE SIMPLE LEAVES

About half of all trees in the region fall into this category, with either thin *deciduous* leaves or ± leathery *evergreen* foliage.

23. THORNY TREES

Only seven trees found wild in the PNW (see also Plates 20 and 22) regularly bear woody thorns or sharp-tipped spur branches. These five species have simple foliage, three bundle scars, and white springtime flowers. In addition, Russian-olive (Plate 32), with silvery foliage, sometimes bears thorns. Canyon Live Oak (Plate 27) and English Holly (Plate 39) may have prickly leaves.

Hawthorns are shrubs or small trees with dense foliage. Thorns *slender,* 1"- 2" long, mostly *not* bearing buds or leaves and occurring on *both* twigs and older wood. Leaf bases *V-shaped;* spur branches mostly *absent.* Fruits small, applelike, mostly *several-seeded,* summer-winter. Favored by songbirds as nest sites. May invade pastures. Many species shrubby. Some used in landscaping.

BLACK HAWTHORN *Crataegus douglasii* Lindl.
The most common hawthorn in much of the West. Foliage 1"- 4" long, *coarsely double-toothed* or irregularly shallow-lobed, and mostly *hairless.* Thorns *1/3"- 1"* long. Mature fruits *black.* Height to 25'. N. New Mexico and cen. California to cen. British Columbia and se. Alaska.

COLUMBIA HAWTHORN *Crataegus columbiana* How.
Much like Black Hawthorn but leaves 1"- 3" long, and *± hairy.* Thorns *1 1/2"- 3"* long. Mature fruits *dark red.* To 16' tall. From California to s. British Columbia, mostly east of the Cascades.

English Hawthorn (*C. monogyna* Jacquin), with foliage deeply lobed and thorns only 3/8" long, also frequently to escapes to the wild.

OREGON (PACIFIC) CRABAPPLE *Malus fusca* (Raf.) Schneid.
A tree of *western* slopes with leaves 2"- 3 1/2" in length, *narrow,* often long-pointed, *sharply and ± coarsely single- or double-toothed,* sometimes shallowly lobed, the bases *U-shaped or square,* and ± hairy. Spur branches *present* on branchlets are often sharp-tipped but *not* slender. Mature fruits pink, *several-seeded,* August-September. To 30' in height and 10" in diameter. From n. California to s. Alaska.

KLAMATH PLUM *Prunus subcordata* Benth.
Leaves 1"- 2 3/4" long, often nearly round, *sharply single-toothed,* with *bases U- to heart-shaped.* Spur branches *stout.* Fruits dark red or purple, tart, *single-seeded,* summer. Height to 25'. Found from n. California and the cen. Sierra to nw. Oregon. A thorny form of **Garden Plum** (*P. domestica* L.) is similar but with leaves 2"- 4" long, *narrowly short-pointed,* and teeth *rounded.* Said to grow wild in w. Idaho and perhaps elsewhere.

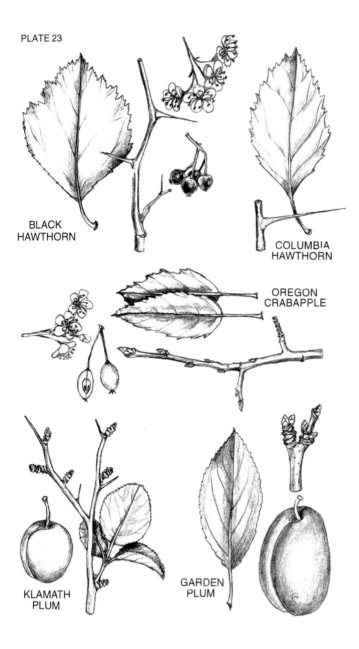

PLATE 23

BLACK
HAWTHORN

COLUMBIA
HAWTHORN

OREGON
CRABAPPLE

KLAMATH
PLUM

GARDEN
PLUM

24. LEAVES FAN-VEINED

These trees have three or more main veins meeting at the leaf bases. Some poplars (Plate 25) also may show such venation. The last two species of this plate are *evergreen* with *even-based, fine-toothed* foliage, *hairless* twigs, *solid* pith, and only *one* bundle scar. They *lack* knobby trunk bark.

NETLEAF HACKBERRY *Celtis reticulata* Torr.

A tree with ± smooth trunk marked by prominent *warty knobs* (photo p. 55). Leaves are *deciduous, sandpaper-textured* above, *net-veined* beneath, *uneven-based,* and short-stalked.They are 2"- 3" long, triangular, and mostly with teeth *few to none.* Twigs are *brown, rounded* and *hairy,* pith is *chambered* (or solid at least at the leaf nodes), and bundle scars are *three.* Flowers are inconspicuous, spring; fruits are small, brown, *one-seeded* spheres with a thin, ± sweet covering, autumn. Height to 50'; diameter to 2'. Dry slopes and streamsides, local from s. Idaho to ne. Washington. Sometimes called Western Hackberry or Sugarberry. Indian-plum (Plate 40), the only other tree in the region with chambered pith, has smooth leaves without teeth.

SNOWBRUSH CEANOTHUS *Ceanothus velutinus* Hook.

Typically a shrub throughout much of the West, a form of this species (var. *hookeri* M. Johnston) grows to be a tree up to 20 ft. tall in the coastal ranges from cen. Calif. to cen. British Columbia. Leaves *evergreen,* thick, gummy, *spicy-aromatic, 2"- 5"* long, broadly oval, dark green, *shiny* above, lighter and *hairless* beneath, long-stalked, and mostly rounded at *both* ends. Twigs *brown, rounded.* Flowers small, *white,* in dense ± cylindrical, 2"- 4" long, twig-end clusters, June-July; fruits black, several-seeded, and sticky, July-November. Height to 20'. Thickets and open woods, Also called Sticky-laurel, Mountain-balm, and Varnishleaf Ceanothus.

BLUEBLOSSOM CEANOTHUS
Ceanothus thyrsiflorus Eschsch.

Like Snowbrush Ceanothus but with leaves *1"- 2 1/2"* long, narrow to wide, sometimes pointed. Twigs *green, angled* or ridged. Flowers mostly *blue,* April-June; fruits July-December. Height to 20'. Forests and chaparral on coastal slopes from s. California to sw. Oregon. Elk and deer browse the twigs. The flowers reportedly will make a soapy lather.

PLATE 24

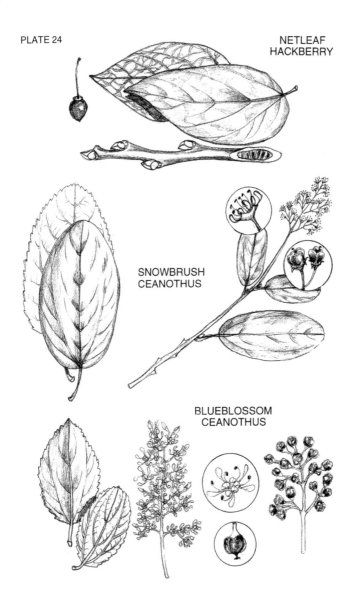

NETLEAF
HACKBERRY

SNOWBRUSH
CEANOTHUS

BLUEBLOSSOM
CEANOTHUS

25. POPLARS: Aspen and Cottonwoods

Though with different common names, these are related species. Leaves are *long-stalked, ± triangular,* and frequently with several main veins meeting at the base (but see Narrowleaf Cottonwood). The *lowest bud scale lies directly above the leaf scar.* Bundle scars three; spur branches occasional. Flowers in *catkins;* fruits fluffy, *cottonlike.* Trunks often smooth and whitish when young.

QUAKING ASPEN *Populus tremuloides* Michx.

Leafstalks are *flattened,* causing foliage to flutter in a breeze. Leaves are 2"- 6" long with *nearly circular, fine-toothed* blades that become golden in autumn. Winter end bud *shiny* but not sticky and only *1/4"- 3/8"* long. Young bark *greenish-yellow to chalk white.* Height to 75'. A widespread tree over North America, ranging even into n. cen. Alaska and n. Yukon. Fast-growing and readily invades burned or cleared areas. Spreading mostly by root sprouts, some groves are estimated to have survived for 10,000 years (far longer than other trees traditionally recognized as being long-lived). See Paper Birch, Pl. 33.

BLACK COTTONWOOD

Populus balsamifera var. *trichocarpa* (Torr. & Gray) Brayshaw Leaves 4"- 8" long, triangular, *fine-toothed,* dark green above, mostly *silver-white* beneath, leafbase glands frequent. Leafstalks *not* flat. Twigs brownish; end bud 3/4"- 7/8" long, *gummy,* and *aromatic* when crushed. Fruit capsules ± hairless, 3-parted. Height to 165', diameter to 3' (9'). Floodplains, from sw. Alaska to nw. Mexico and inland to e-cen. British Columbia, sw. Alberta, s-cen. Montana, n. Utah, and the Sierra Nevada. Wood used for paper pulp, boxes, and rough lumber. Now a subspecies of **Balsam Poplar** (*P. balsamifera* L.) which ranges east across Canada and n. U.S. from most of Alaska and Yukon to cen. Colorado with leaves only pale beneath and fruit capsules ± hairy, 2-parted. **Eastern Cottonwood** (*P. deltoides* Bartr.) extends east from sw. Alberta /w. Montana with wide, *heart-shaped* leaves, *glands* at the leaf base, and stalks *flattened* .

NARROWLEAF COTTONWOOD *Populus angustifolia* James

Tree almost *willowlike* and thriving on moist ground. Leaves are *narrow* but, unlike willows (see Plates 28-31), the buds are *several-scaled.* Leaves are 3"- 5" in length, feather-veined, and without glands. Stalks *about 1"* long, *flattened only near the blade.* Winter end bud *1/4"-1/2"* long, *gummy,* and *spicy.* Upper bark whitish. Height to 60'; diameter to 18". From n. cen. Mexico to se. Oregon, cen. Idaho, nw. Montana, sw. Alberta.

White Poplar (*P. alba* L.), a European import established locally, has leaves 2"- 6" long, either *deeply lobed or triangular.* Foliage, twigs, and buds are *white-woolly.* **Lombardy Poplar** (*P. nigra* var. *italica* Muenchh.), also of Old World origin, is a tall, thin, *columnar* tree with aspenlike foliage, often planted.

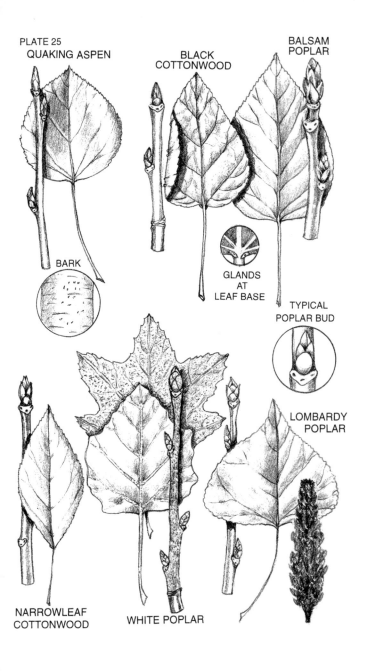

PLATE 25
QUAKING ASPEN

BLACK
COTTONWOOD

BALSAM
POPLAR

BARK

GLANDS
AT
LEAF BASE

TYPICAL
POPLAR BUD

LOMBARDY
POPLAR

NARROWLEAF
COTTONWOOD

WHITE POPLAR

26. END BUDS CLUSTERED and ACORN FRUITS: Oaks I

Regardless of foliage, oaks (Plates 26-27) can be identified by *end buds clustered* at the twig tips. Oaks also have *more than three* bundle scars per leaf scar and, of course, bear *acorn* fruits. In late spring, male blossoms occur in slender, *drooping* catkins several inches long. Female flowers are small and unobtrusive. Acorns, green at first, become brown when mature. They are held in basal *cups* that, nevertheless, are commonly described as either bowl-shaped or saucerlike. Pacific Bayberry (Plate 32), Golden Chinkapin (Plate 32), Cultivated Cherries (Plate 36), Fire Cherry (Plate 37), Cascara Buckthorn (Plate 38), and Indian-plum (Plate 40) also may have buds clustered at or near the twig ends but other distinctive field marks are evident.

An oak species is often classified as a member of either the red or white oak group. The lobe and leaf tips of red oaks have protruding hairlike *bristles* that are lacking in white oaks. Also, the acorns of red oaks take two years to mature while those of white oaks require only one. This causes mature red oaks usually to have developing acorns on the twigs *plus* older ones on the branchlets. White oak acorns, on the other hand, grow *only* on the twigs. In addition, the inner surface of the shells (not cups) of red oak acorns are *hairy* while those of white oaks are *not.* The meat of red oak acorns, too, usually contains much tannic acid and is bitter, while that of white oaks is light-colored and more edible. Canyon Live Oak (Plate 27) is an exception to some of these guidelines.

Oaks are often valuable timber trees. Their acorns are essential in the diets of deer, squirrels, and many other wildlife species. Acorns also once served as important foods for Native Americans. Even the bitter acorns of red oaks were rendered edible by pounding the kernels and treating the flour with hot water. Reportedly, early settlers used dried acorn shells as a coffee substitute.

CALIFORNIA BLACK OAK *Quercus kelloggii* Newb.
A deciduous member of the red oak group with leaves 4"- 7" long, deeply lobed, *bristle-tipped*, the stalks *1"- 2"* long. Buds about *1/4"* in length, and *hairless.* Acorns *1"- 1 1/2"* long, the cups *bowl-shaped.* Trunk *dark.* Height to 75' (95'); diameter to 3' (4'). Coast ranges and the Sierra Nevada from s. California to sw. Oregon. Similar species from the eastern United States, often planted for landscaping, may be distinguished by their smaller acorns and either less-deeply lobed leaves or shorter leafstalks.

PLATE 26

CALIFORNIA BLACK OAK

27. END BUDS CLUSTERED and ACORN FRUITS: Oaks II

The following trees, in sequence, are (1) a lobed-leaved member of the white oak group, (2) an *intermediate oak* with mixed white oak /red oak features, and (3) a non-*Quercus* species that bears acorns. The last two are evergreen. See Plate 26 for characteristics of oaks and oak groups.

OREGON OAK *Quercus garryana* Doug. ex Hook.
A deciduous oak with smooth-edged *deeply-lobed* foliage *not* bristle-tipped. Leaves 4"- 6" in length, somewhat *leathery, glossy* above, usually *hairy* beneath. Buds *1/4"- 1/2"* long and *hairy.* Trunk bark *light gray.* Acorns 3/4"- 1 1/2" long, with *shallow* cups. Height 40'- 65' (90'). Mostly west of the Cascades from cen. California to s. Vancouver Island, also the Sierra Nevada. Named for Nicholas Garry, an early Hudson's Bay Company officer and botanist. Also called Oregon White Oak and Garry Oak.

CANYON LIVE OAK *Quercus chrysolepis* Liebm.
Called a live oak because of its *evergreen* foliage, the leaves are *thick,* rather *leathery,* and often *hollylike* with edges either smooth or somewhat prickly. Leaves only *1"- 2 1/2"* long, rather waxy, and often whitened or *yellowish* beneath. Side veins mostly *parallel.* Acorn cups deep, thick-walled, and often *gold-hairy.* Though the fruits mature in *one* year on the twigs like white oaks, the inner acorn shells are *hairy* like red oaks. Trunk bark *grayish.* To 60' tall, canyons and moist open slopes from nw. Mexico and s. Arizona to sw. Oregon. The dense wood once was made into wedges and mauls (heavy hammers) to split logs. Maul Oak is an alternate name. Golden Chinkapin (Plate 32) has yellow leaf undersides; English Holly (Plate 39) may have prickly foliage.

TANOAK *Lithocarpus densiflorus* (Hook. and Arn.) Rehd.
Unlike true oaks (genus *Quercus*), male catkins are *upright* with the small female blossoms at the bases of male catkins. A large tree whose *evergreen* leaves are *2"- 5"* long, whitish- to brownish-hairy beneath, and *sharp-toothed* but not prickly. Side veins are ± *parallel.* Twigs and buds *yellow-hairy.* Acorns develop over a 2-year period in *saucerlike* cups decorated with *narrow, spreading* scales. Trunk *dark.* Height 50'-100' (150'); diameter 1'- 3' (6'). Mainly coastal, from s. California to sw. Oregon and local in the n. and cen. Sierra Nevada. Also called Tanbark-oak or merely Tanbark. Southern Asia is home to many *Lithocarpus* species.

PLATE 27

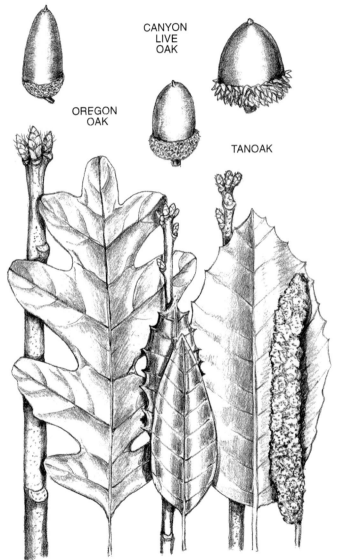

CANYON
LIVE
OAK

OREGON
OAK

TANOAK

28. BUDS WITH ONE SCALE: Willows I

Though some willows can be recognized by their *slender* leaves, others have wider foliage [and some non-willows (Plate 32) also have narrow leaves]. The field mark that best identifies willows (Plates 28-31) regardless of leaf shape is the *single, smooth, caplike scale* covering the bud (use lens). Willows have three bundle scars per leaf scar and flowers /fruits in slender, dry, caterpillarlike catkins. Most willows grow on moist soils. Many are shrubs. Vegetative characters are variable; hybrids are common; identification is often difficult.

The twigs of nearly all willows are eaten by deer, elk, moose, caribou, rabbits, hares, and many rodents. Salicin, a chemical derived from willow bark, is the original substance from which aspirin was developed.

The trees of this plate have leaves *very narrow* (8-15 times longer than wide). Except for some Sandbar and Northwest willows, the leaf edges are *fine-toothed.* Leaf bases are mostly *V-shaped* and leaf stalks are short or lacking. Most species have gray-green foliage.

SANDBAR WILLOW *Salix exigua* Nutt.
A streamside species with *very* narrow, long-pointed leaves 3"- 6" long and only *1/8"- 1/2"* wide. Leaf undersides and twigs often *white-hairy.* Leaf teeth wide, often *few,* rarely none. To 20' tall. Transcontinental, extending west to the e. slopes of the Cascade /Coast ranges and north to cen. Alaska and cen. Yukon. The long twigs and branchlets are used in basket-making. Hinds Willow (*S. hindsiana* Benth.) is no longer differentiated.

RIVER WILLOW *Salix fluviatilis* Nutt.
Like Sandbar Willow but leaves *yellow-green, 3"- 6"* long, *5/16"- 1/2"* wide, and *silky-hairy to whitish-hairless* beneath. Twigs ± hairless, often white-powdered. Recorded from the lower Columbia and Willamette river valleys.

NORTHWEST WILLOW *Salix sessilifolia* Nutt.
Resembling River Willow but foliage shorter and wider (3-10 times longer than wide), sometimes with *a few teeth* mainly above the middle. Leaves 1 1/4"- 4" long, *1/2"- 1 1/4"* wide, *broadest near the middle,* silky- or *long-hairy* on both surfaces, and whitened beneath. Twigs long-hairy, often whitened. River sandbars, sw. Oregon to sw. British Columbia.

Weeping Willow (*Salix babylonica* L.), often planted, has *extremely long* twigs /branchlets that *hang vertically,* often sweeping the ground. Leaves 1"- 5" long, 1/4"- 1/2" wide, *long-pointed,* hairless or silky, *glands often present* on upper leafstalk. Leafstalks to 1/4" in length. Height 25'-50' (60'); diameter 1'- 3'. Of Chinese origin.

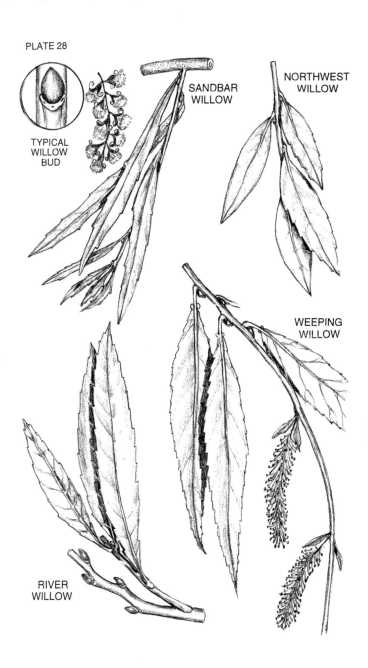

PLATE 28

TYPICAL
WILLOW
BUD

SANDBAR
WILLOW

NORTHWEST
WILLOW

WEEPING
WILLOW

RIVER
WILLOW

29. BUDS WITH ONE SCALE: Willows II

These species have leaves of *medium* width (5-7 times longer than wide). Foliage of the first two is *without* teeth, *short-pointed*, and bases *V-shaped*. The others have leaves *fine-toothed*, hairless, whitened beneath, bases mostly *U-shaped*, stalks mainly 1/2"- 3/4" long and without glands (use lens). Twigs mainly hairless; winter buds mostly *under 1/8"* long. Northwest (Plate 28) and Littletree (Plate 31) willows sometimes also have leaves of medium width. Narrowleaf Cottonwood (Plate 25), too, is quite willowlike.

GEYER WILLOW *Salix geyeriana* Anderss.
Leaves *silky-hairy,* only *1"- 3"* long, *3/8"- 1/2"* wide, whitened beneath, and stalks 1/8"-3/8" long. Twigs somewhat reddish, often with a whitish powder. Height to 15'. Western mountains south from s. British Columbia. Karl Geyer, a German botanist, collected plants in the West during the 1840s.

ARROYO WILLOW *Salix lasiolepis* Benth.
Leaves shiny, rather *leathery,* somewhat thickened, the edges ± rolled under, *2"- 5"* long, *1/2"- 1"* wide, ± hairy beneath, and stalks 1/8"- 1/4" long. Twigs yellowish; buds *over 1/4"* long. Height to 30'. Mainly Pacific slope of California /sw. Oregon; local north to n. Washington and w. Idaho.

PACIFIC WILLOW *S. lucida* ssp. *lasiandra* (Benth.) E. Murray
Leaves shiny, dark green above, *long-pointed,* and with *glands present* on upper leafstalk (use lens). Leaves 2"- 6" long, 1/2"- 1" wide, stipules common. Buds *over 1/4"* in length. Height to 60'. Distributed from s. California and New Mexico to cen. Alaska, cen. Yukon, and e. Saskatchewan. Useful for making charcoal. Previously named *S. lasiandra.*

PEACHLEAF WILLOW *Salix amygdaloides* Anderss.
Also with foliage *long-pointed*, the leaves 3'- 7" long, 3/4"- 1 1/4" wide, *dull-surfaced,* yellow-green above, stipules present or not. Twigs brown to *orange, ± drooping.* Height to 80'. From e. North America to se. British Columbia, Idaho, and e. Oregon.

MACKENZIE WILLOW *Salix prolixa* Anderss.
Leaves *short-pointed*, dark green above, the bases U- or ± *heart-shaped.* Leaves 2 1/2"- 4" long, 5/8"- 1 1/2" wide, stipules frequent. Leafstalks 1/4"- 3/4" in length. Twigs *red-brown* to yellowish, sometimes hairy. Height to 20'. Mainly inland from nw. Wyoming to cen. British Columbia, se. Yukon, and ne. Alberta. Found also in the Sierra Nevada and local in Oregon. Also known as *S. mackenzieana,* and sometimes listed as a variety of *S. rigida.*

PLATE 29

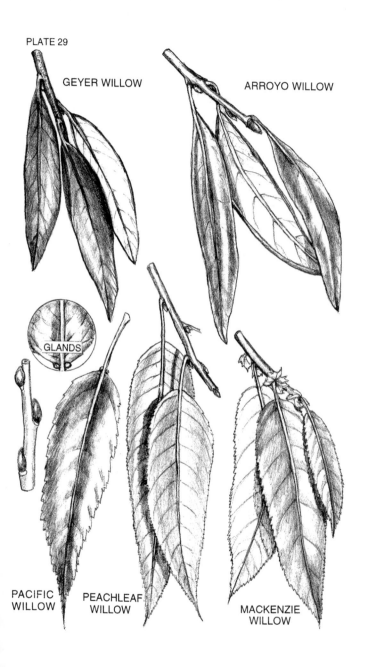

GEYER WILLOW

ARROYO WILLOW

GLANDS

PACIFIC WILLOW

PEACHLEAF WILLOW

MACKENZIE WILLOW

30. BUDS WITH ONE SCALE: Willows III

These willows have *wide* leaves (only 2-4 times longer than wide) and are found south of the U.S.- Canada boundary *as well as* north to Alaska. (Willows of Plate 31 occur in the PNW *north of the international border.*) Foliage is *without* glands and mainly *V-based.* Height to 20'- 30'. Northwest Willow (Plate 28) also sometimes has wide leaves. See Plate 28 for characterics of willows as a group. Narrowleaf Cottonwood (Plate 25) is also willowlike.

SITKA WILLOW *Salix sitchensis* Bong.
A willow with leaves *dull* above, densely *shiny-velvety* beneath, *short-pointed,* widest *above the middle,* mostly without teeth, and the edges strongly *rolled under.* Foliage *2"- 4"* long, 3/4"- 1 1/2" wide, and short-pointed or blunt. Twigs mostly *white-hairy.* Coastal, n. California to s. Alaska; inland to e. Oregon, nw. Montana, and cen. British Columbia.

SCOULER WILLOW *Salix scouleriana* Hook.
This species also has leaf edges ± *rolled under* and mostly not toothed. Leaves *2"- 5"* long, *1/2"- 1 1/2"* wide, more or less wavy-edged, mostly *blunt,* widest *near the tip*, and somewhat *whitened* beneath. Twigs ± hairy. Found over most of the Pacific Northwest, often on rather dry sites. John Scouler, a Scottish physician, studied plants along the Pacific Coast in the early 19th century.

HOOKER WILLOW *Salix hookeriana* Hook.
A coastal willow, the leaves /twigs ± *white-woolly.* Foliage 2"- 5" long, 1"- 2" wide, *widest near the tip, ± blunt* or short-pointed, *U-shaped* at the base, smooth-edged or ± wavy-toothed. Twigs stout. Near the ocean, from n. California. to s. Alaska. Inner bark fibrous and used by native peoples for making lines, nets, etc. William J. Hooker was a British botanist in early America.

BEBB WILLOW *Salix bebbiana* Sarg.
Leaves 2"- 3" long, 1/2"- 1" wide, whitish- or *gray-hairy,* tapered at *both* ends, and teeth *coarse* or none. Twigs *gray-hairy* and tending to branch at wide angles from the branchlets. Wood used for charcoal and long withes (twigs /branchlets) may be woven into baskets. Throughout the Rocky Mountains; transcontinental in the north, ranging east from cen. Alaska.

PLATE 30

SITKA WILLOW

SCOULER WILLOW

HOOKER WILLOW

BEBB WILLOW

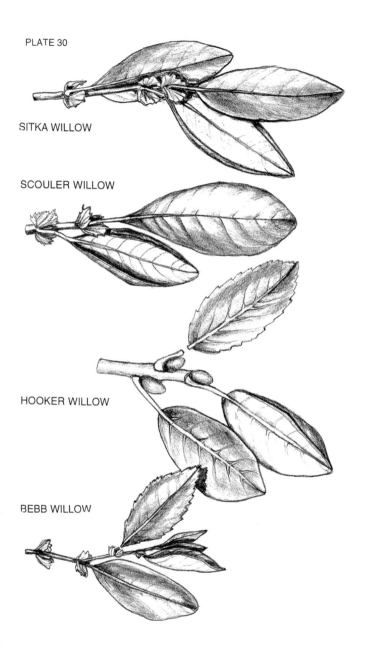

31. BUDS WITH ONE SCALE: Willows IV

Like the trees of Plate 30, these northern willows mostly have *wide* foliage (leaf length only 2-4 times width). *All occur in British Columbia, Yukon, or Alaska*; none of these four species is found in the Washington /Oregon /Idaho /nw. Montana region (but see Pussy Willow). The first two species do not grow wild anywhere in the lower 48 states. Leaves are short-pointed. To 20'- 30' tall.

FELTLEAF WILLOW *Salix alaxensis* (Anderss.) Cov.
   The most far-northern of PNW tree willows. Foliage (and usually twigs) *densely white-woolly.* Leaves 2"- 4" long, 1/2"- 1 1/2" wide, yellow-green, *without* teeth, bases V-shaped, stipules small and slim. N. British Columbia, Yukon, and most of mainland Alaska.

LITTLETREE WILLOW *Salix arbusculoides* Anderss.
   Leaves 1"- 3" long , 3/8"- 3/4" wide (but foliage sometimes 5-6 times longer than wide), dark green, *fine-toothed, silver-hairy beneath,* bases V-shaped, without stipules. Twigs hairy or not. Common as a shrub or small tree from Hudson Bay west to cen. British Columbia, Yukon, and much of interior Alaska.

BALSAM WILLOW *Salix pyrifolia* Anderss.
   An aromatic willow. Foliage with *firlike odor* when crushed. Leaves 1"- 5" long, 1"- 1 1/2" wide, dark green, whitened beneath, *fine-toothed,* mostly *hairless,* U-based, stipules small or absent. Twigs hairless. From e. Canada and n. Wisconsin /Minnesota to e. cen. British Columbia and e. Yukon.

PUSSY WILLOW *Salix discolor* Muhl.
   A willow with blue-green leaves mostly *coarse-toothed, hairless,* and whitened beneath. Foliage 2"- 5" long, 1/2"- 1 1/2" wide, U- or V-based, and stipules often large. Twigs hairy or not. A species primarily of e. North America but with its western range including nearly all of e. British Columbia. Also local in w. cen. Idaho.

PLATE 31

FELTLEAF
WILLOW

LITTLETREE
WILLOW

BALSAM
WILLOW

PUSSY
WILLOW

32. NON-WILLOWS WITH NARROW LEAVES

The first three trees have leathery, *evergreen* leaves. Only Pacific Bayberry may have leaves toothed. Most have leaf bases V-shaped and buds scaly. Some cherries (Plate 35) also have narrow foliage. None of these species has the single, caplike bud scale of willows.

PACIFIC BAYBERRY *Myrica californica* Cham.

A *coastal* species with leaves 3"- 4" long, 1/2"- 1" wide, hairless, short-pointed, widest *above the middle*, *spicy-scented* when crushed, with *coarse teeth* or none and black or yellow *resin-dots* beneath (use lens). Leaves and buds *crowded* near the twig tips. Flowers greenish, in 1" long catkins; fruits 1/8"-1/4" in diameter, *white-waxy*. Height to 35'. Near the ocean, from s. California to sw. British Columbia.

CALIFORNIA BAY *Umbellularia californica* (Hook. & Arn.) Nutt.

Leaves 3"- 5" long, *not* toothed, and *either* short-pointed or with blunt tips. Foliage green and shiny above, *pale* beneath, and strongly *aromatic* when crushed. Twigs also green and spicy-scented. Buds small, *without* scales. Flowers small, yellow, in umbrellalike groups, December-April. Fruits purplish, oval, 3/4"- 1" long, *smooth*, with a large seed, October-winter. Height 30'- 80'. From s. California to sw. Oregon and in the Sierra Nevada. Dried leaves often used to flavor food. Squirrels and jays consume the fruits. Wood used for fine furniture and art objects. Also called Oregon-myrtle or California-laurel.

GOLDEN CHINKAPIN *Chrysolepis chrysophylla* (Doug. ex Hook.) Hjelmq.

With leaves much like those of California Bay, the foliage of this species is *golden-yellow* beneath, *not* spicy, and with *sharp* tips. Twigs also yellow; buds grouped near the twig ends. Flowers whitish, tiny, May-June. Fruits 4-parted *prickly burs*, 1"- 1 1/2" long, that contain 1-3 angled nuts. Height 20'- 80' (130'); diameter 1'- 3' (4'). Coastal regions, from cen. California to the Puget Sound region. Mule deer browse the foliage. Previously known as *Castanopsis chrysophylla*. Canyon Live Oak (Plate 27), also with end buds clustered and foliage yellowed beneath, has small leaves often prickly-edged.

RUSSIAN-OLIVE *Elaeagnus angustifolius* L.

A Eurasian import widely planted for ornament and as a drought-resistant windbreak. Leaves *deciduous*, 1"- 4" long, 1/2"- 1" wide, short-pointed, U- or V-based, green above, and *silver-scaly* beneath. Plant often thorny, twigs *silver-white*. Flowers yellowish, spring; fruits egg-shaped, ± fleshy, silver-red to white. Height to 25'. Often called Oleaster. Fruits eaten by many birds and mammals. Silver Buffaloberry (Plate 20), also silvery, has opposite leaves. When thorns are present, compare Plate 23.

PLATE 32

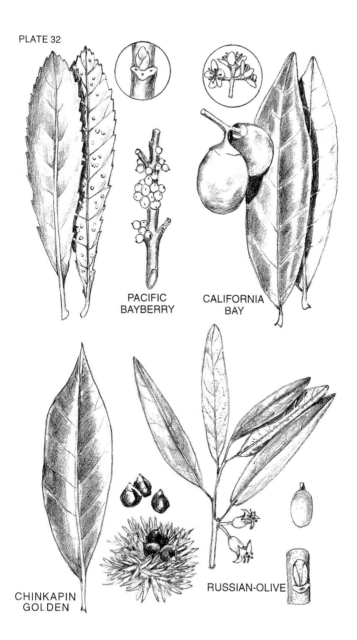

PACIFIC
BAYBERRY

CALIFORNIA
BAY

CHINKAPIN
GOLDEN

RUSSIAN-OLIVE

33. LEAVES DOUBLE-TOOTHED:
Birches and California Hazelnut

Birches have leaves whose major teeth also are toothed. They also have smooth bark with *crowded* horizontal streaks, buds with only *2-3 scales,* spur branches present, twigs mostly rough-warty, and tiny, dry fruits in slim, *non-woody* catkins. California Hazelnut has double-toothed and alderlike foliage, but is otherwise not birchlike and also lacks the hairless leaves and stalked buds of most alders (Plate 34). Mountain Alder (Plate 34) has *scattered* bark streaks.

PAPER (WHITE) BIRCH *Betula papyrifera* Marsh

A gray- or *white-trunked* tree with *dull, papery, peeling* outer bark marked with thin horizontal lines. Leaves mostly *over 2"* long, ± short-pointed, *± hairy* beneath, and with *5-9* pairs of side veins. Twigs *smooth* or slightly rough-glandular. Immature trunk smooth, red-brown. Height 70'- 80' (120'). Transcontinental to s. Alaska and nw. Washington. Also ne. Washington ton to nw. Montana. Often called Canoe Birch. Quaking Aspen (Plate 25) has whitish bark but lacks bark peels and differs otherwise. **Resin Birch** (*B. neoalaskana* Sarg.) with young trunk brown, leaves ± hairless, and twigs with *many large* resin-glands, ranges from n. cen. Alaska to nw. Ontario. **Kenai Birch** (*B. kenaica* Evans), also with young trunk brown, has leaves less than 2" long, 2-6 pairs of side veins, and *few small* twig-glands. It occurs from w..to e. cen. Alaska.

WEEPING (EUROPEAN WHITE) BIRCH *Betula pendula* Roth

Much like Paper Birch but with twigs *pendent* and the trunk bark *glossy, black-fissured* at the base, sometimes peeling in strips. Leaves *1"- 3"* long, *± hairless,* and (like the twigs) often with small resin-dots. Twigs *hairless,* ± smooth. Height to 40'. A landscape tree established in the wild in Washington state.

WATER BIRCH *Betula occidentalis* Hook.

A birch with *red-brown, shiny* trunk marked by *white* transverse streaks. Leaves *1"- 3"* long, *short-pointed,* often heart-shaped, and with *4-5* pairs of side veins. Twigs *rough-warty, hairless*; buds pointed. Height to 40'. Local throughout mountains of the American West, and from ne. and s. cen. British Columbia to w. Ontario. See cherries, Plate 36, also with young brown bark.

CALIFORNIA HAZELNUT

Corylus cornuta ssp. *californica* (A. DC.) E. Murray

A *hairy-leaved* plant with foliage *heart-shaped* or nearly circular. Twigs usually *hairy;* buds *blunt* with *4-6* scales, the lowest ones *paired.* Fruits are tasty nuts in *beaked* husks 1"- 2" long. Trunk brown, unmarked. Height to 25'. From n. California and the Sierra Nevada to s. and cen. British Columbia. Related to Beaked Hazelnut of the East and to European filbert.

PLATE 33

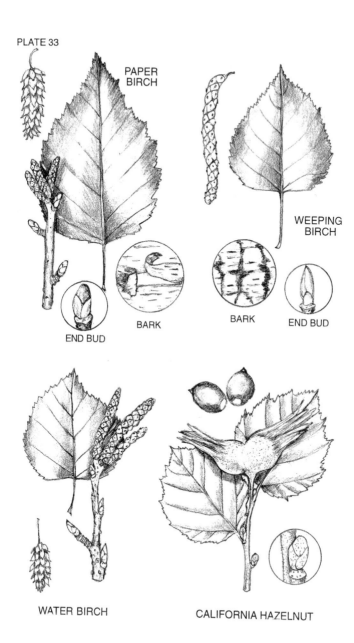

PAPER BIRCH

WEEPING BIRCH

END BUD

BARK

BARK

END BUD

WATER BIRCH

CALIFORNIA HAZELNUT

34. LEAVES mostly DOUBLE-TOOTHED/ CATKINS LIKE SMALL PINE CONES: Alders

Mature female alder catkins are brown and woody *like inch-long pine cones.* Foliage is mostly *double-toothed,* short-pointed, *hairless,* 2"- 6" long, with main veins parallel. Buds are mostly *stalked, reddish, blunt,* 1/4"-3/8" long, with *2-3* scales *not* overlapping. Cone stalks are mostly *1/16" thick* and *shorter than* the cones. Mostly on damp sites. Most leaves of Plates 33-36 are also double-toothed. California Hazelnut (Plate 33) has leaves alderlike.

Alders are among the few non-legumes with root nodules that support nitrogen-fixing (soil-enriching) bacteria. Powdered alder bark makes an orange-red dye and is said to control both diarrhea and external bleeding. Deer, beavers, and porcupines eat the twigs or inner bark; several grouse species feed on the buds.

RED ALDER *Alnus rubra* Bong.

Our largest alder. Leaves with edges *narrowly rolled under* (use lens), coarsely toothed, and *10-15* pairs of side veins. Cones *1/2"- 1"* in length. Trunk bark thin, fine-lined, *gray mottled with white.* Wood becomes red-brown. Height 40'- 60' (100'); diameter 1'-3' (6'). Mostly coastal, cen. California to Alaska panhandle; local in ne. Washington /n. Idaho. A fast-growing species, the lumber used for furniture and construction.

MOUNTAIN ALDER

Alnus incana ssp. *tenuifolia* (Nutt.) Breitung.

Leaves with deep teeth, *flat* edges, and *6-9* pairs of side veins. Trunk bark gray, often with short, *scattered,* horizontal lines. Cones 3/8"- 5/8" long. Height to 30'. Mountains, from the Sierra Nevada and s. Rockies to w. cen. Alaska and n. Yukon. Formerly named *Alnus tenuifolia* . Also called Thinleaf Alder.

WHITE ALDER *Alnus rhombifolia* Nutt.

Foliage variable, the leaf edges finely *single-toothed,* faintly double-toothed, or merely wavy-edged. Leaves with *9-12* pairs of major side veins. Buds *1/4"-3/8"* long. Trunk dark, scaly. Height to 60'. Streambanks and dry slopes to 8000' elevation. From s. California and w. cen. Nevada to w. cen. Washingon. Also in the ne. Washington /n. Idaho /nw. Montana region.

SITKA ALDER

A. viridis ssp. *sinuata* (Regel) A. Löve & D. Löve.

Leaf undersides ± *shiny-sticky,* side veins *6-10* pairs, teeth *finely long-pointed* (use lens). Unlike our other alders, mature buds are *sharply pointed,* resinous, *not* stalked, and with *4-6* scales. Cone stalks *thin* (1/32") and *as long as* the cones. Trunk gray, smooth. Height to 35'; diameter to 10". Snowslide areas, stream banks, nw. California and cen. Montana to sw. and cen. Alaska and n. Yukon. Earlier named *A. sinuata* or *A. crispa* var. *sinuata.*

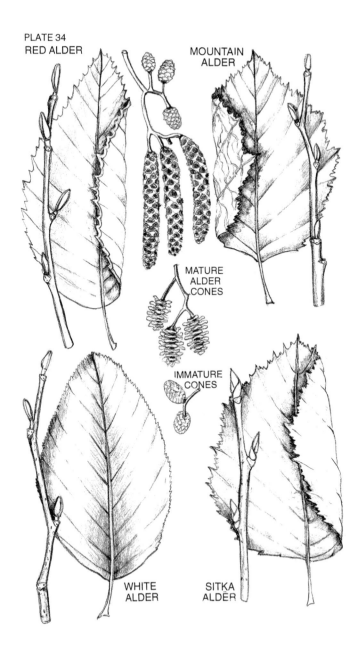

PLATE 34
RED ALDER

MOUNTAIN ALDER

MATURE ALDER CONES

IMMATURE CONES

WHITE ALDER

SITKA ALDER

35. LEAVES MOSTLY DOUBLE-TOOTHED, uneven-based, and rough-hairy: Elms

Elms are trees with dark furrowed trunks, 4-8 scales per bud, three bundle scars, small flowers that lack petals, and small, winged, papery, 1-seeded, almost-circular fruits. Most have foliage *double-toothed,* decidedly *uneven-based,* and *rough-hairy.* Only Siberian Elm is single-toothed and ± even-based. Buds are ± pointed. In the spring, flowers and fruits are produced before the leaves are fully grown.

The inner bark of the roots, trunk, branches, and twigs of elms is *tough and fibrous.* Starting with a small cut, lengths of fibrous materials can be pulled from the root or branch. This serves as a useful identification mark and also can offer materials for emergency use as cordage, snares, fishing lines, or nets. Elm wood is difficult to split.

Of the many elm species that occur in eastern North America and Eurasia, several have been introduced into the Pacific Northwest.

AMERICAN ELM *Ulmus americana* L.
Introduced from the East some years ago, this graceful tree with divided trunk and vase-shaped outline, has been decimated in its home territory by "Dutch" elm disease, a fungus. Leaves 4"- 6" long, *smooth* or only slightly sandpapery above, and with bases *uneven.* Twigs hairless; buds with *6-8* scales, *brown with dark edges.*

ENGLISH ELM *Ulmus minor* Miller
A tree much like American Elm but *single-trunked* with the leaves *rough-hairy* above, and only *2"- 3"* long. Buds *almost black.* Often with many twig suckers along the trunk and large branches. Reported to have escaped to the wild near Victoria, Vancouver Island, British Columbia, and perhaps elsewhere. Often named *Ulmus procera* Salisb.

SIBERIAN ELM *Ulmus pumila* L.
Leaves *single-toothed* and *not* markedly asymmetrical at the base. Buds *small,* 4-scaled,and ± blunt; flower buds *enlarged,* nearly *black,* conspicuous in late winter. An import from Asia, often planted for windbreaks and occasionally escaping. Often called Chinese Elm, but that name is more properly applied to *U. parviflora* Jacq. naturalized mainly in the se. United States.

PLATE 35

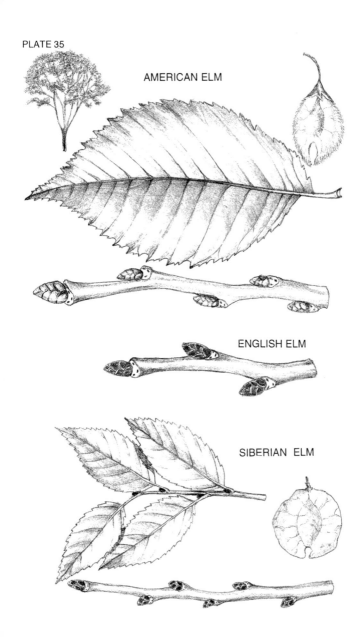

AMERICAN ELM

ENGLISH ELM

SIBERIAN ELM

36. LEAVES DOUBLE-TOOTHED: CULTIVATED CHERRIES

Cherries have trunks mostly marked by numerous thin *horizontal lines* (see also birches, Plate 33, and Mountain Alder, Plate 34). Leaves are short- or long-pointed and 2"- 6" long. Buds have *several* scales and leaf bases or leafstalks mostly bear one or two tiny *glands.* Spur branches are *present* and flowers are in *short, rounded* groups, *except* in Chokecherry (Plate 37). Twigs are mostly hairless with a *sour* or almond odor when broken. Springtime flowers are small and white; fruits are spherical, *fleshy, single-seeded.* The thorny plums (Plate 23) are related members of the genus.

These cultivated European imports have escaped to the wild in some localities of the Pacific Northwest. Unlike the wild cherries of Plate 37, the foliage of these trees is *double-* rather than single-toothed and leaves /buds are often clustered at the twig tip.

Most birches (Plate 33) also have double-toothed foliage, spur branches, and at least the younger bark with horizontal lines but they have only 2-3 bud scales and none has leafstalk glands or cherry-odored twigs. Oregon Crabapple (Plate 23), California Hazelnut (Plate 33), many alders (Plate 34), and most elms (Plate 35) also have double-toothed foliage.

SWEET (MAZZARD) CHERRY *Prunus avium* (L.) L.
A rather tall tree with a *single* main trunk. Bark *red-brown* and smooth. Leaves *± sharply toothed,* often long-pointed, and with *10-14* pairs of side veins. Spur branches *leafless.* Fruits red to black, sweet, June-July. Height 30'- 50' (75'); diameter 1'- 2' (3'). The parent of many of the sweeter kinds of garden cherries. Also called Gean and Bird Cherry.

SOUR CHERRY *Prunus cerasus* L.
This species usually *lacks* a distinct central trunk. Bark is *gray* and much cracked. The foliage has *coarse, blunt* teeth and *6-8* pairs of lateral veins. Spur branches *leafy.* Fruits red, sour, July-August. Height 20'- 30'; diameter 10"- 12". Many tart-flavored cultivated cherries have been bred from this species. A preferred cherry for pies. Believed to have originated in w. Asia.

PLATE 36

SWEET CHERRY

GLANDS

SOUR CHERRY

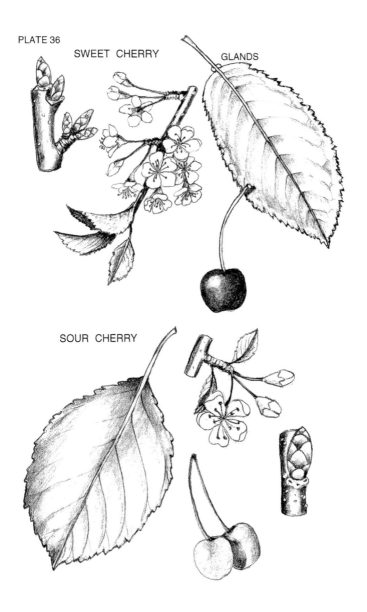

37. LEAVES SINGLE-TOOTHED:
Wild Cherries and Maheleb

These cherries have finely *single-toothed* and mostly sharp-tipped foliage (see Plate 36 for other characteristics of cherries). *Except* for Chokecherry, spur branches are *present* and flowers are in *short, rounded* groups. Many trees of other alternate-leaved groups (Plates 21-32, 34, 35, 38, 39) also may have leaves single-toothed.

BITTER CHERRY *Prunus emarginata* (Hook.) Walp.
Leaves 1"- 3" long, sometimes narrow, usually with tips *round-pointed,* and teeth rather *blunt.* Fruits 1/4"- 1/3" across, red to black. Height 60'- 80' (100'). North from the southwestern United States to s. British Columbia and nw. Montana. Sometimes in thickets. Many animals eat the fruits despite their bitter taste; mule deer browse the twigs.

FIRE (PIN) CHERRY *Prunus pensylvanica* L. f.
A cherry with *narrow, sharp-toothed* leaves 2"- 5" long. Buds with *pointed* scales *crowded toward the twig tips* (and on spur branches). Fruits red. Height 10'- 30' (40'). From cent. British Columbia to Newfoundland and the s. Appalachians. Often invades burned areas. Fruits sour, used in jellies and cough syrup. Fruits also eaten by several grouse species; deer, moose, cottontail rabbits, and beavers browse the twigs and bark.

MAHALEB CHERRY *Prunus mahaleb* L.
The only PNW cherry with *hairy* twigs and small (1'- 3" long) leaves that are often *almost circular,* ± heart-shaped at the base, with teeth *rounded,* and *aromatic* when crushed. Of Eurasian origin, sometimes planted and locally wild. The name is of Arabic origin. Fruits dark; yield a violet dye and an oil used to fix perfumes. Also called Perfumed Cherry.

CHOKE CHERRY *Prunus virginiana* var. *demissa* (Nutt.) Torr.
Distributed throughout the West, this transcontinental cherry ranges from s. California, w. Texas, and Virginia to w. Washington, cen. British Columbia, and Newfoundland. Foliage 2"- 5" long, *egg-shaped,* and *sharply* toothed. Leafstalks often reddish. Spur branches *absent;* flower/fruit clusters 2"- 4" long and *slender.* Fruits purple to black. Height to 30', thickets and woods. Many birds and mammals consume the tart fruits; they are sometimes used for pies and jelly.

PLATE 37

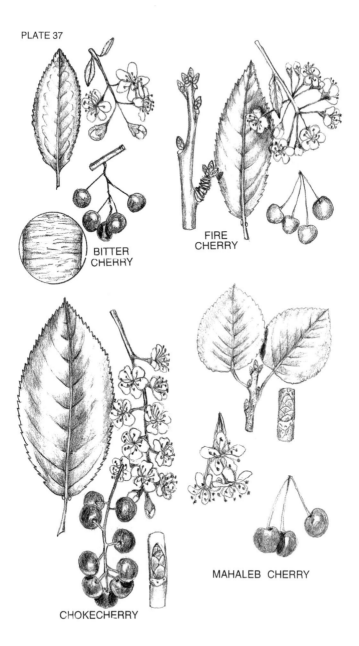

BITTER
CHERRY

FIRE
CHERRY

CHOKECHERRY

MAHALEB CHERRY

38. LEAVES MOSTLY SINGLE-TOOTHED:
Serviceberries / Cascara

These species differ from those of Plate 37 in that horizontal lines on the trunk, glands on the leafstalk, and the distinctive odor from broken twigs are all *lacking*. They *do* have hairless twigs and three bundle scars per leaf scar but their fruits are *several-seeded* and their other characteristics are unlike those of cherries. Cascara Buckthorn may be without leaf teeth; the seedlings are reported often to hold their leaves in winter. Klamath Plum (Plate 23) also is single-toothed with sharp spur branches.

WESTERN SERVICEBERRY (Saskatoon Juneberry)
Amelanchier alnifolia (Nutt.) Nutt.

A small tree or shrub with leaves *1"- 3"* long and *nearly circular.* There are 3-20 pairs of *coarse teeth* mainly *toward the leaf tip* and *7-9* pairs of side veins mostly branched and *curved.* Leafstalks *1/2"- 1"* long. Buds purplish and *scaly;* spur branches usually *present.* Flowers attractive, *white,* clustered, the petals 3/8"- 5/8" long; April-June. Fruits juicy, tasty, *purplish,* and 1/4"- 1/2" wide; June-August. Height to 42'. Found from nw. California, nw. New Mexico and Minnesota to n. cen. Alaska and ne. Manitoba. The origin and meaning of the Serviceberry name are uncertain (unless derived from Sorbusberry, see Plate 21). Western Juneberry and Alderleaf Juneberry are other names.

UTAH JUNEBERRY *Amelanchier utahensis* Koehne

A shrub or low tree similar to Western Serviceberry but leaves only *1/2"- 1 1/4"* long, including *1/4"- 1/2"* stalks. Flower petals and fruits also small, the former only 1/8"- 1/4" long and the latter just 1/8"- 1/4" in diameter. Scattered localities, slopes and canyons throughout the American West north to s. Oregon, cen. Idaho and sw. Montana.

CASCARA BUCKTHORN *Rhamnus purshiana* DC

Well-known in the Pacific Northwest; the bark is commonly harvested for use as a tonic and laxative. Leaves *3"- 6"* long, 1"- 2 1/2" wide, *fine-toothed* or sometimes without teeth, and with *10-15* pairs of prominent *straight, parallel,* and *opposite* lateral veins. Foliage and buds tend to be bunched near the twig tips (leaves sometimes nearly opposite). Leaf tips *short-pointed* or blunt. Buds rusty-hairy, *without* scales; spur branches *lacking.* Stump sprouts common. Thorns are lacking, despite the name. Flowers small, *greenish,* May-July; fruits fleshy, *black,* July-September. Trunk bark light gray, smooth. Height to 40'. Occurs mostly west of the Cascades from cen. California to w. cen. British Columbia and again in n. Idaho /nw. Montana /se. British Columbia and nearby. Fruits eaten by many wildlife species; mule deer consume the twigs. California Buckthorn (Pl. 39) is related.

PLATE 38

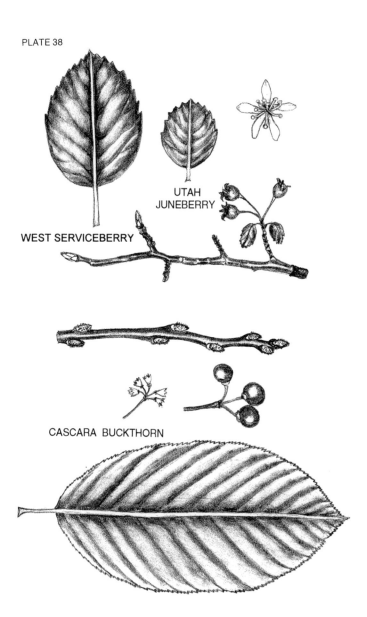

UTAH
JUNEBERRY

WEST SERVICEBERRY

CASCARA BUCKTHORN

39. EVERGREEN TREES WITH LEAVES TOOTHED OR SOMETIMES TOOTHED

Birchleaf Cercocarpus, and usually European Holly, have *single-toothed* foliage. The other two species have leaves mostly smooth-edged but sometimes toothed. Pacific Bayberry (Plate 32) and Whiteleaf Manzanita (Plate 40), also evergreen, are toothed or not.

BIRCHLEAF CERCOCARPUS *Cercocarpus betuloides* Torr. & Gray
The long *feathery tails* on tiny fruits are most attractive. Leaves *3/4"- 1 1/2"* in length, *parallel-veined, wedge-based,* often velvet-hairy beneath, and toothed *above the middle.* Buds *scaly;* spur branches *frequent.* Flowers greenish, 1/4" wide in small groups, March-May; fruits single-seeded, narrow, dry, 1/2" long, with a plume 1 1/2"- 4" long. Height to 25'. Chapparal, from nw. Mexico and cen. Arizona along the coast to sw. Oregon and locally in the Sierra. Wood is often brownish and used in woodworking. It is heavy and will not float soon after being cut. Also called Mountain-mahogany, but not related to tropical mahoganies. The name Cercocarpus is based on the Greek for "tailed fruit". In the absence of fruits, compare California Buckthorn. Curlleaf Cercocarpus (Plate 40) is related.

ENGLISH HOLLY *Ilex aquifolium* L.
Spreading in PNW, with leaves mostly *prickly-edged, green* on both surfaces, and 3/4"- 1 1/2" long. Fruits *red,* fleshy. See Canyon Live Oak, Plate 27.

CALIFORNIA BUCKTHORN *Rhamnus californica* Eschsch.
With variable foliage and *rarely* attaining tree size, this species has leaves 2"- 4" long and often *whitish* beneath. Leaves have 5-11 pairs of *parallel* veins, either U- or V-shaped bases. They are often fine-toothed (rarely with rather coarse teeth) and occasionally opposite. Buds hairy, *without* scales. Spur branches *lacking.* Flowers greenish, March-April; fruits *black,* juicy, several-seeded, August-September. To 15' tall. Ranging mainly from n. Baja California to extreme sw. Oregon, local elsewhere in the Southwest. Frequently called California Coffeeberry.

PACIFIC MADRONE *Arbutus menziesii* Pursh
Well-known by the thin, *smooth, reddish-brown* bark on the upper trunk and large branches (see also Whiteleaf Manzanita, Plate 40), that may often peel to show grayish-yellow underbark. Leaves 4"- 6" long, sometimes with fine teeth. Leaf bases U-, or occasionally, heart-shaped. Buds *scaly,* hairless. Flowers small, white, bell-shaped, in branched groups, March-May; fruits red to orange, spherical, 1/4"- 1/2" wide, June-winter. Height 25'- 80' (125'); diameter 2'- 3' (5'). Mostly coastal, from s. California to sw. British Columbia. Fruits are consumed by doves, bandtailed pigeons, and ringtails. Deer browse the twigs. Bees collect nectar.

PLATE 39

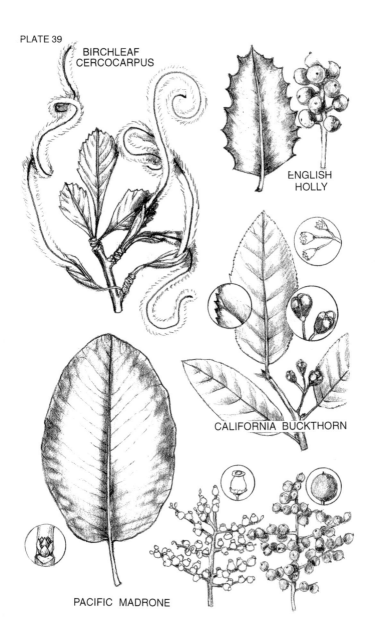

BIRCHLEAF
CERCOCARPUS

ENGLISH
HOLLY

CALIFORNIA BUCKTHORN

PACIFIC MADRONE

40. TREES WITH LEAVES NOT TOOTHED

The first species has deciduous foliage; the last three are evergreen (see also Plate 32). Some trees of Plates 22, 24, 27-32, 38, and 39 also may lack leaf teeth.

INDIAN-PLUM *Oemleria cerasiformis* (Hook. & Arn.) Landon

Usually a shrub, occasionally treelike. Leaves 2"- 4" long, faintly wavy-edged or teeth *lacking*, short-pointed, base *narrowly V-shaped*, fine-hairy beneath (use lens), often clustered near the twig ends. Twigs purplish, hairless; pith finely *chambered;* buds ± blunt, green, usually 3-scaled, sometimes stalked; bundle scars three. Trunk bark without horizontal markings. Flowers whitish, in narrow, pendent clusters, March-April; fruits thinly fleshy, one-seeded. Height 5'- 15' (22'). Western slopes of the Sierra Nevada to w. Washington and sw. British Columbia. Also called Osoberry. Former generic names *Osmoronia* and *Nuttallia* are often seen.

CURLLEAF CERCOCARPUS *Cercocarpus ledifolius* Nutt.

A shrub or small tree of mountain slopes throughout the American West. Leaves only *1/2"- 1 1/2"* long, pointed at both ends, short-stalked, sometimes hairy beneath, and with edges *curled under.* Spur branches *common.* Flowers without petals and inconspicuous. Fruits tiny but with interesting *feathery tails* 2"- 3" long. Mainly dry slopes, from s. California and sw. Colorado to se.Washingon /cen. Idaho /sw. Montana. The heavy brown heartwood will not float but makes nice turned objects and leads to the alternate name of Mountain-mahogany. Mule deer browse the leaves and twigs. Birchleaf Cercocarpus (Plate 39) is related.

PACIFIC RHODODENDRON
Rhododendron macrophyllum D. Don

A small tree or shrub of coastal areas and Cascades with leaves *3"- 6"* (10") long, 1"- 2" (2 1/2") wide, hairless, *pointed at both ends,* the edges *rolled under.* Flowers showy, *1"- 2" long,* pink-purple (occasionally white), in large groups, May-June; fruits slim, dry, brown capsules. To 25' tall. Foliage poisonous to sheep. From cent. Calif. to nw. Oregon and Puget Sound.

WHITELEAF MANZANITA *Arctostaphylos viscida* C. Parry

Rarely reaching tree size, the trunk is *smooth, bare,* and *red-brown,* much the color and texture of Pacific Madrone (Plate 39). Leaves *1"- 2"* long, ± egg-shaped, mostly hairless, rarely fine-toothed, and somewhat whitened. Flowers urn-shaped, pink or white, 1/4"- 3/8" long; fruits spherical, 1/4"- 3/8" wide, fleshy or leathery, mostly reddish. Distributed from n. California to sw. Oregon. Also in the Sierra Nevada.

PLATE 40

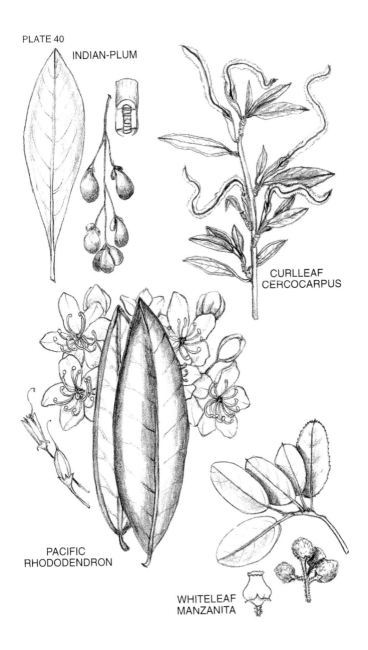

INDIAN-PLUM

CURLLEAF
CERCOCARPUS

PACIFIC
RHODODENDRON

WHITELEAF
MANZANITA

KEY TO TREES IN LEAFLESS CONDITION

Each key item is a couplet. Compare the unknown specimen with the first pair of choices. Select the alternative that agrees with the specimen and proceed to the couplet number indicated. Repeat until a final determination is reached. Use a lens when necessary. In addition to these broadleaf trees, larches (Plate 5) are conifers that lose their needles in winter.

1. *Leaf scars opposite* (Sections II and III of text). **2**
1. Leaf scars alternate (Sections IV and V of text) **10**

    2. Leaf scars meeting in raised points.   **Ashleaf Maple Pl. 15**
    2. Leaf scars not meeting in raised points. **3**

3. Buds without scales, hairy, opposite mostly only near
    twig tips.   **Cascara Buckthorn Pl. 38**
3. Buds scaly. **4**

    4. Bud scales 2 (or 4), edges meeting. **5**
    4. Bud scales several, overlapping, or smooth and granular. **8**

5. Bundle scar one.   **Buffaloberry, Burningbush Pl. 20**
5. Bundle scars three. **6**

    6. Pith brown.   **Pacific and Smooth Dogwoods Pl. 19**
    6. Pith white. **7**

7. Twig leaf scars raised; fruits fleshy, spherical.

                                      Dogwoods Pl.19
7. Twig leaf scars not raised; fruits dry, winged.   **Maples Pl. 17**

    8. Twigs stout; pith wide; central end bud missing, a single pair
       of buds usually present at twig tips.   **Elderberries Pl.16**
    8. Twigs slender; pith narrow; central end bud present, often
       flanked by side buds. **9**

9. Buds scaly; fruits in winged pairs.   **Maples Pls. 17, 18**
9. Buds smooth, granular; fruits single-winged.

                                     Oregon Ash Pl. 15

    10. *Leaf scars alternate,* thorns present. **11**
    10. *Leaf scars alternate,* thorns absent. **13**

11. Thorns paired.   **Black Locust Pl. 22**
11. Thorns single. **12.**

    12. Twigs silvery.   **Russian-olive Pl. 32**
    12. Twigs not silvery.
    Hawthorns, Oregon Crabapple, Klamath Plum Pl. 23

13. *Trees with one of the following (a-i) unique characteristics:*
13. *Trees lacking these distinctive (a-i) characteristics.* **14**

    a. Buds clustered at the twig tips (see also some Cherries
       Pls. 36, 37).   **Oaks Pls. 26-27**
    b. Buds without scales.   **Cascara Buckthorn Pl. 38**
    c. Buds with a single, smooth, caplike scale.
                           Willows Pls. 28-31
    d. Twigs silvery.   **Russian-olive Pl. 32**
    e. Catkins like inch-long pine cones, usually present;
       buds blunt with 2-3 scales not overlapping.   **Alders Pl. 34**
    f. Pith chambered or at least blocked at the nodes.
          Netleaf Hackberry Pl. 24, Indian-plum Pl. 40
    g. Leaf scars 1/4"- 3/4" deep, triangular; twigs thick,
       pith solid.   **Tree-of-Heaven Pl. 22**
    h. Leaf scars U-shaped, more or less surrounding the buds,
       fruits small, dry, clustered, red-hairy, pith wide, twigs
       flat-sided, bundle scars many.   **Smooth Sumac 22**
    i. Inner bark of small branches can be peeled in fibrous
       strips when cut.   **Elms Pl. 35**

    14. Buds with lowermost scale centered directly above the
       leaf scar; bark often smooth and greenish on young trunk
       and branches; spur branches occasional.   **Poplars Pl. 25**
    14. Bud scales and trunk bark otherwise. **15.**

15. Spur branches absent; buds few-scaled, the lowest scales
    larger and paired; twigs usually hairy; fruits nuts.
                    California Hazelnut Pl. 33
15. Spur branches usually present (also Poplars Pl. 25). **16**

    16. Trunk marked with short horizontal lines; bundle scars 3,
       fruits dry or fleshy, one-seeded. **17.**
    16. Trunk bark without horizontal lines; bundle scars 3 or 5,
       fruits fleshy, several-seeded. **18.**

17. Buds with 2-3 scales; broken twigs without an almond or sour
    odor; fruits dry catkins (see also Mountain Alder, Pl. 34).
                        Birches Pl. 33
17. Buds with 4-6 scales; broken twigs often with an almond or
    sour odor; fruits juicy spheres.   **Cherries Pl. 36, 37**

    18. Buds stout, reddish; bundle scars 3-5; fruits orange or red.
                     Mountain-ashes Pl. 21
    18. Buds long-pointed, purplish, scales often twisted and
       with black notched tips, second bud scale usually less
       than half length of bud; bundle scars 3; fruits purple.
                      Juneberries Pl. 38

REFERENCES

Arno, Stephen F. and Ramona P. Hammerly. 1977. *Northwest Trees.* The Mountaineers, Seattle, Washington.

Brayshaw, T. Christopher. 1996. *Trees and Shrubs of British Columbia.* UBC Press, Vancouver.

Cody, William J. 1996. *Flora of the Yukon Territory.* NRC Reserch Press, Ottawa

Davis, Ray J. 1952. *Flora of Idaho.* W. C. Brown Company, Dubuque, Iowa.

Hickman, James C. (edit.) 1993. *The Jepson Manual: Highter Plants of California.* Berkeley, Univ. Calif. Press.

Hitchcock, C. Leo and Arthur Cronquist. 1973. *Flora of the Pacific Northwest.* Seattle, Univ. Wash. Press.

Hitchcock, C. Leo, Arthur Cronquist, Marion Ownbey, J. W. Thompson. 1955, 1959, 1961, 1964, 1969. *Vascular Plants of the Pacific Northwest. Parts 1-5.* Seattle, Univ. Wash. Press.

Little, Elbert L. 1971. *Atlas of United States Trees,* vol. 1. U.S. Forest Service, Department of Agriculture, Misc. Publ. 1146.

_____ 1979.*Checklist of United States Trees.* U.S Forest Service, Department of Agriculture, Agri. Handbook 541.

McMinn, Howard E. and Evelyn Maino. 1980. *An Illustrated Manual of Pacific Coast Trees.* 2nd ed. Berkeley, Univ. Calif. Press.

Morin, Nancy R. (edit.). 1993, 1997. *Flora of North America,* vols. 2 and 3. New York, Oxford, Oxford Univ. Press.

Peck, Morton Eaton. 1961. *A Manual of Higher Plants of Oregon.* Oregon State University Press, Corvallis, Oregon.

Petrides, George A. and Olivia Petrides. 1992. *A Field Guide to Western Trees.* Houghton Mifflin Co., Boston, Massachusetts .

Piper, Charles V. 1906. *Flora of the State of Washington.* Contrib. of United States National Herbarium, Vol. XI, Washington, D.C.

Piper, Charles V. and R. Kent Beattie. 1915. *Flora of the Northwest Coast.* New Era Printing Company, Lancaster, Pa.

Pojar, Jim and Andy MacKinnon. 1994. *Plants of Coastal British Columbia.* B. C. Ministry of Forests and Lone Pine Publishing, Vancouver, British Columbia.

Ross, Charles R. 1978, 1985. *Trees to Know in Oregon.* Extension Bull. 697, Oregon State University, Corvallis, Oregon.

Viereck, Leslie A. and Elbert L. Little, Jr. 1972. *Alaska Trees and Shrubs.* U. S. Dept. of Agriculture Handbook 410, Washington.

Welsh, Stanley L. 1974. *Anderson's Flora of Alaska and Adjacent Parts of Canada.* Brigham Young University Press, Provo, Utah.

INDEX TO PLATES

102

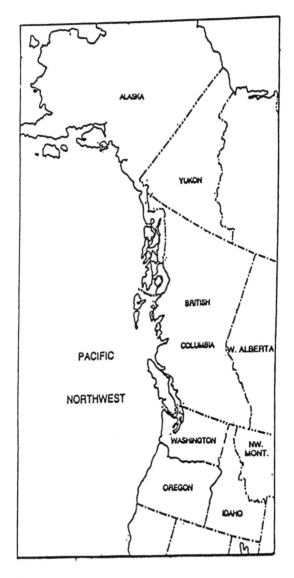

ALASKA

YUKON

BRITISH

COLUMBIA   W. ALBERTA

PACIFIC

NORTHWEST

WASHINGTON   NW.
MONT.

OREGON

IDAHO

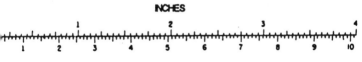

INCHES

CENTIMETERS

   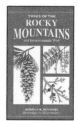